FACING HEWITT

Symposium of a Champion

By Scoop Malinowski

Introduction

Lleyton Hewitt has been described as "a lion", "a computer", "a boxer", "a beast." Racing around the court with the fury of an attacking tiger, wielding his Yonex like a light saber against Darth Vader, Hewitt strikes a unique figure. Propelled by an extraordinary drive and desire, the fiery Australian counterpuncher has achieved a Hall of Fame worthy career since first qualifying for the Australian Open at age fifteen in 1997. In almost two decades on the ATP World Tour, Hewitt, the youngest player to ever achieve the ATP top ranking, has won over 600 ATP matches, Wimbledon, the U.S. Open, Davis Cup, 29 singles titles overall, and over $20,000,000.

In this book, over 50 ATP players recall their memories about competing against Hewitt, revealing fascinating insights and details about one of the most dynamic gladiators in tennis history...

Thanks and gratitudes go out to so many people who helped make this project possible. All the players who graciously took the time to talk about playing Lleyton Hewitt, including Taylor Dent, Jan-Michael Gambill, Nikolay Davydenko, Jason Stoltenberg, Richard Krajicek, Alex Corretja, Jeff Tarango, Mats Wilander, Gael Monfils, Guillermo Canas and so many others. Many ATP Tour and media mavens were also extremely helpful, such as Greg Sharko, Paul MacPherson, Jeanmarie Daly, Tim Curry, Chris Widmaier, Lisa Franson, Sam Henderson, Kayla Holst, Christopher Clarey, Vivienne Christie, Lisa Franson, Clive Brunskill, Anne Marie McLaughlin, Tony Driscoll, asap sports, etc.

"A fighter needs dragons to slay." *--Michael Bentt*

Chapter 1: Talking About Lleyton Hewitt

"It was unbelievable to see him up close..."

Mats Wilander talks about Hewitt in a special interview at the 2014 Sony Open: "I would think the first time I saw him was at the U.S. Open when he won it. I didn't really see him when he was young. When he was a sixteen year old, I wasn't much into tennis then. I remember watching him at the U.S. Open."

Question: Were you impressed by his style of play in his best years?

Mats Wilander: "Not on TV, no, not on TV, I wasn't that impressed by him. But I was Davis Cup captain for Sweden and we played Australia in Malmo, him and Philippoussis played. And that was unbelievable...to see him up close. Because it's hard to see on TV why he's so good. They hit the ball so hard but when you see him live you realize how well he moves, how he competes. So yeah, it was extremely impressive."

Question: Which guys from Sweden did Hewitt beat in that tie?

Mats Wilander: "He beat Thomas Enqvist and he beat Jonas Bjorkman."

Question: Lasting memory or image of Hewitt on or off court, interviewing him, imitating your Vicht?

Mats Wilander: "Yeah, of course, him imitating, yeah because, Vicht, he calls it 'Come On.' But it's the same thing. I think my memory of him is at the Australian Open, for sure, of the late, late night matches that he'd always get involved in. They were special. Any time Lleyton plays at night at the Australian Open, I'm watching every point. It's great, it's great to watch him."

Question: Does he remind you of you?

Mats Wilander: "Mmmm...a little bit. Yeah, I guess. He's more vocal, obviously. But he competes really hard. I mean, he might be the best in terms of the ones that compete the best out of any player of all time. Him and Nadal I would think. They'd be the two that stand out."

Question: If they were equal size and strength, who do you think would win that, Hewitt or Nadal? If they were both heavyweights? Because Hewitt is more of a middleweight.

Mats Wilander: "It's a little different. Hewitt is somehow hanging in the game with a style that is sort of a little bit outdated. But he's just perfect proof that if you're a competitor and you play every situation as hard as you can, there's always room for the smaller guys in tennis. And I think he's a perfect example that you don't have to be a certain size. You have to have a certain size heart, that's all."

Question: Does the Vicht translate to mean 'Come on' in

Swedish?

Mats Wilander: "Not 'come on.' It means, 'Yeah, sure. Sure.'"

Question: Do you think the Vicht was the origin of the 'Come on?'

Mats Wilander: "Well, that is it. Of course, a hundred percent. Not one percent, a hundred percent. The first time it was ever seen was Australian Open in '88 when I was playing. I was playing quarters, semis and finals. Niclas Kroon was there. And Peter Lundgren was there. They played the tournament and they lost. And they said, 'Hey, we're gonna go home.' I was hanging out with them every day. So, 'Come on, don't go home, man.' In Swedish. And they said, 'We'll stay if you do the Vicht on the court. So then I did the Vicht on court. And they stayed for an extra few days. And then I heard that the pictures in the Australian newspapers were of other Australian athletes doing it. Ian Thorpe was one. Remember him? Swimmer. Another one that got sent to me was a race horse - the owner and jockey standing next to the race horse. And then, before I knew it, Lleyton was doing it. So I would think he would have seen it on TV from there. Niclas Kroon always did it. I don't think he would have seen Niclas Kroon do it because he wasn't on TV that much. But he could have seen him do it. But certainly, it's the same thing, of course it is."

Richard Williams (Father/Coach of Venus & Serena Williams):   "He's a great man. Lleyton Hewitt. If he never played and hit another ball, he's a part of history. He's great. Super guy. The operations and the things he's been through...to come back from that...he's one of my heroes. I love Lleyton Hewitt."

Andy Roddick talking about Lleyton Hewitt at the 2012 U.S. Open.

"Oh, man, he's probably the best competitor I played against. It's weird. This year we've probably become friends. At first we probably didn't like each other much, and then it came to the point where we respected each other. Then it was slowly like we kind of each give a little ground and say, How you doing? I'm good. How are you? Okay. Now we'll text each other back and forth after matches and stuff. It's funny, how that's come full circle. I come in today and he's in the throes of a battle. Our lockers are right next to each other. He came in and he was really pumped up. It would be hard for anyone to respect what he's done in this game more than I do."

John Newcombe talks about the teenaged phenom Hewitt at the July tie vs. USA in Boston in 1999.

"He's been part of the Davis Cup sports since he's been fifteen. We've had him at nearly every match since then. So he's really been blooded for this occasion, whenever it came. And I think he thought and we thought it would be maybe some time next year, so it's come a little bit early. But he's been totally prepared, and he's seen a lot and observed a lot and he's a great observer, as people who become champions are. So I think to go back to your question, he's going to be nervous, but it will be a good type of nervous. It will be match nervous and settle down after a couple of games. But he'll probably have to play Pete (Sampras) first up, which is a pretty big thing when you're coming in here for the Davis Cup match."

Carlos Moya: "He's very difficult. He runs like crazy, and all the balls are coming back. Mentally he's the number one. And as I said, maybe he doesn't have the talent of Safin or Kuerten, but mentally he's the number one in the world I would say. He never gives up, and he's always there."

Marat Safin: "He's really consistent, he doesn't lose his mind and he's just playing his game. It's not really impressive game, but he's running, he doesn't make any mistakes, he has really fast hands, fast legs. You cannot play his game. And when he's starting to play his game, it's just baseline, he just kills you. You know, he plays the balls in the right way, in the right place, and it's difficult to play with him, against him from the baseline. He's really, really consistent."

Novak Djokovic after beating Hewitt for the first time at 2007 Wimbledon.

"You need to be physically very ready for him and mentally as well. He doesn't give you free points. You got to earn your points. You got to make a lot of -- you need to be aggressive, but on the other hand you need to stay patient. At U.S. Open last year, in that third round, I didn't recognize myself on the court. I was really trying to make winners out of every position, and he likes that. He likes to play rallies. He likes just hanging in there on the baseline and wait for the opponent to make a mistake. And today was different. Of course from every match you learn something new. I knew I have to be very patient, but on the other hand to try to get to the net more. I managed to do that."

Rod Laver speaks about Hewitt in 2001.

"Lleyton certainly has got a lot of talent. I think his heart is his biggest attribute to making things happen on a court. He is certainly very steady and the one thing that I marvel at is just the way he is able to get to the ball with so much time, which allows him then to have his options open to him whether he wants to go down the line or cross court, so he has got time. So he has got consistency which a lot of players don't have that consistency as groundstrokes."

Andrew Golota, 1988 Olympic bronze medalist boxer and four-time challenger for World Heavyweight titles, discusses which ATP players possess the qualities to become a "champion boxer."

"Everybody has a chance. You've got to be a fighter. McEnroe would play them dirty. He made them lose their focus, that's exactly what he did every time. He's the most distracting guy I've ever seen. Made them lose their focus. He was aggravating people. But I think Andy Roddick. He's the biggest, strongest one I think. He has the fastest serve. Safin — maybe. Hewitt — he looks like a fighter. I think he wants to be a fighter. He acts like a fighter."

Greg Norman: "My favorite players to watch? It depends. I'm a huge Roger fan. I'm a huge Lleyton Hewitt fan. Because I just admire Lleyton's determination and grit, he maximizes everything that he gets out there and puts his best foot forward every time, which is a rare talent indeed."

"In tennis, Lleyton is the most tenacious I've ever seen. There's no quit in him. All the other players don't have any quit in them but Lleyton's sense of awareness of what he wants on the tennis court is just unique and I've got a huge respect for him."

Question: You and Lleyton play golf together. Is his tenacity and intensity on the golf course similar to the way it is on the court?

Greg Norman: "Yeah [smiles]. Yeah, I think we're all that way. No matter what we do – if it's another sport or whether it's scuba diving or something like that, we want to be the best we can be at it. Because it's in our blood. That's our make-up. No matter what challenge we have, same as golf, into sport, into business, we're taking that competitive spirit and edge to it. And you just want to be the best you can at it."

"I call him the epitome of what every young kid should look up to. And you look at his track record... if I was a father of a kid who was six, or eight, or nine years old today, I'd be actually getting them to watch what Lleyton's done. See how his career has gone. The longevity. It's a great testament to an athlete."

Jim Courier describes working with Lleyton Hewitt as a TV analyst.

"Hewitt's loss is Australian fans' gain at the Australian Open. If he loses, he takes a day or two off, then he joins us in the TV booth. He is tremendous as an analyst. First of all, he's playing these guys, so he has unique perspectives. He gets his point across quickly, succinctly and articulately. He's a superstar at commentating as well as a superstar player. He also tells us some things about players that he probably shouldn't. It's interesting to hear him talk about the guys he's played, often it's the guy who he just lost to. It's fascinating. It's made him so much more liked by the public in Australia, much like John McEnroe in this country. It's humanized him."

Jimmy Connors Interview in New York City in 2006 for Tennis Week Magazine.

Speaking of favorite players to watch, you must like to watch Lleyton Hewitt too (Come on!)?

Jimmy Connors: "Yeah, well, yeah, as a grinder. Any time I say grinder, that's kinda my kind of guy [smiles]. But he really, at one time was able to be in every match, and I've seen the last few years — he's struggled a little bit. Maybe that's due to some of the interests he's gone through off the court. But his attitude is one that when he's out on the court, that's his business and that's what he wants to do. And he's willing to put it all on the line. And day after day, that's a hard job."

Alex Corretja talking about Hewitt before the Spain vs. Australia 2000 Davis Cup final in Barcelona.

"I think he's going to be pretty pumped. No matter if I said that he's behaving on the court, from my point of view, wasn't right. I think he knew it already. He knows the way he is. He knows that he likes to make provocations to the other players. There is nothing new. Maybe I'm the first one to say that, but everybody knew it on the Tour. I don't have anything against him like personally. As he said, and I really agree with him, it's as we're playing here Spain against Australia, not Hewitt against Corretja. If we have to face each other, of course it's going to be a big war to play against each other because of the motivation of winning Davis Cup and maybe afterwards because of our personal situation. But I don't think now we are not going to be friends. Before we weren't friends anyway."

Pete Sampras after losing to Hewitt in the U.S. Open final.

"Well, the reason I wasn't quite that sharp is because of the way he was returning, the way he was passing. You know, every time I made a second serve, he made me play. I was hitting low volleys. It's hard to do that three sets, let alone. I just -- the harder I served, the more I put into it, the better he returned. He's got the best return in the game, the best wheels in the game. He possesses now a much better serve. He's a great player. You'll see him contending here for the next ten years."

Nick Kyrgios talking about Hewitt at the 2014 Sarasota Challenger.

"In Davis Cup I've practiced with Hewitt the week before. I train with him as well. He's a great guy. He's one person who I think his actions speak louder than his words. When he's on the court he goes a hundred percent every ball every time he steps out there. So I think being out on the court with him sort of raises your game as well."

Chapter 2:   Facing Lleyton Hewitt

ATP Players describe their memories of competing against Lleyton Hewitt...

"I tell the players: You'll hear a lot of applause in your life, but none will mean more to you than that applause - from your peers. I hope each of you hears that at the end."

--Andre Agassi

Any avid tennis player may wonder what it feels like to play against the best in the world. You get a satisfactory sense of what it must be like to battle Lleyton Hewitt from watching on TV or being there live at an ATP World Tour event. Your eyes can easily appreciate the burning intensity, the flashes of speed, the magic wand-precise shot-making, and the finely-tuned defensive skills.

Your ears enjoy the rhythmic sounds of the contact points, the cat-like footwork and of course those infamous (and oft controversial) roars of emotion, or as some suggest, intimidation.

But what does it really feel like to compete against someone as tenacious and fiery, as talented and concentrated as Lleyton Hewitt?

The people who are best qualified to contemplate this inquiry are the special group of professional players who have actually had the opportunity to engage in court combat with this unique colossus named Lleyton Hewitt...

"He's a great example for the rest of the players."

Rafael Nadal: "I admire him when I was a kid and saw him on the TV. I like his character. He's always fighting for every ball. He always gives everything on the court. He's a good example of how to fight in the tennis court. When I was younger I remember very good battles against him. In Australia I lost twice but one in three very close sets and another one in five sets. It was great memories and especially playing at his home. So I always have good memories of the matches against him."

Question: Describe the feeling of facing Hewitt and does he remind you of yourself more than anybody else in terms of competitive spirit?

Rafael Nadal: "Well, I don't know about that. I think he's a great champion for a lot of players after winning a lot of things as he did, and having a lot of physical problems he's able to keep competing with unbelievable spirit, great motivation. He's able to come back after important injuries. So that's a great example for the rest of the players. I am happy to see him playing well again."

Nadal leads series 7-4

2004   Australian Open   R32   Hewitt 76 76 62
2004   Toronto   R64   Hewitt   16 64 62
2005   Australian Open   R16   Hewitt 75 36   16 76 62
2006   Roland Garos   R 16   Nadal   62 57 64 62
2006   Queens   QF   Hewitt   36 63 ret.
2007   Hamburg   SF   Nadal   26 63 75
2007   Roland Garros   R16   Nadal 63 61 76
2008   Beijing Olympics   R32   Nadal 61   62
2009   Roland Garros   R32   Nadal 61   63 61
2010   Roland Garros   R32   Nadal   63 64 63

2014   Miami Masters   R64   Nadal 61   63

"I love players who play with the heart and have a passion for the game."

Jonas Bjorkman: "I could never beat him. I think I'm 0-8 or 0-9. But we had good matches, close matches. But his play was not good for me. Everything I gave was what he liked. It was a bad match-up."

Question: What surprised you about him?

Jonas Bjorkman: "He didn't surprise me much. He's such a great competitor. That was the thing. In my situation, I wanted to come to the net and he wanted almost everyone to come to the net. And he passed you. What he did well, I think when he played his best, was that he never tried to pass you on the first shot. He always tried to put it low in the middle. To be left to pass you on the second one. And he had such great passing shots. It was tough for a player like me to become stronger than him in the match. I was close a few times but not good enough."

Question: Your most memorable match with Hewitt?

Jonas Bjorkman: "We had a big battle in Australian Open. I think that was fun in a way. Because I had all my Swedish support obviously there. And he was playing in front of his home crowd. The atmosphere was great. I think I lost in five. But it was a great match."

Question: Do you have good relations with Hewitt off the court?

Jonas Bjorkman: "Yeah. I love players who play with the heart, have passion for the game. Even now when he's out there playing, it's great to watch him play. He doesn't have to play but he still loves it. And that's what is so great about it. For juniors now he's a great inspiration to watch him play. We had him in Stockholm last year at our event. There was a lot of juniors there watching. And I was happy that we managed to get him to Stockholm. To show how good he is."

Hewitt leads series 7-0

```
1998   Sydney   R32   Hewitt 63 67 64
2001   Australian Open   R128    Hewitt   75 46 26 63 62
2001   Davis Cup SF    Hewitt   46 64 76 76
2002   Rome Masters   R64   Hewitt 62 63
2002   Wimbledon   R128    Hewitt 64 75 61
2004   Hamburg Masters   R64    Hewitt 60 76
2008   Olympics Beijing    R64   Hewitt 75 76
```

"It was very difficult to win points against him."

Alex Corretja: "Well, he was a great fighter. Very tough opponent. Very fast on the court. Good returns. Good eyes. Good footwork. Very sound mentally. Very, very solid. He improved a lot on every surface and he is a very, very tough guy to play against actually."

Question: Did anything surprise you about playing Hewitt?

Alex Corretja: "Well, it was very difficult to win points against him because he didn't make too many mistakes. He had a great backhand, good forehand. He had good returns, good first serve, good second serve, so he was very complete."

Question: Most memorable match with Hewitt?

Alex Corretja: "Well, we had some matches. And some of them were not good for me and some of them were better."

Question: Did you get along with him off court, did you ever practice together?

Alex Corretja: "No, I haven't practiced with him much. But no problem with him. He's a good guy and that's it."

Hewitt vs. Corretja series tied 3-3

2000   Sydney   SF Hewitt   64 64
2000   Australian Open   R64 Hewitt 60 60 61
2000   Masters Cup Lisbon   RR   Corretja   36 76 63
2001   Rome Masters   R16   Corretja 76 64
2001   World Team Cup Dusseldorf   RR   Corretja   36 62 63
2003   Scottsdale   QF Hewitt 64 62

"Lleyton breaks your will. He loves that part of it."

Jeff Tarango: "I played Hewitt at the French Open in
2000. A three- hour, three-set match. I can still vividly
remember how exhausted I was both physically and
mentally. I immediately nicknamed him 'The Mongoose'
because Lleyton is the type of player and person that grabs
onto you as an opponent and engages you as if he will not
give an inch or a mental break until he has drained and beat
you."

"I had chances to win both the first two sets and the rallies
we had were more like an 'ultra marathon training camp'
than an actual match. We had at least fifty points that were
over forty-ball rallies and he won most of them - and then
to add insult to injury or my pumping lungs, as the case
was, to hear a 'COME ON' - and it was a long, shriek of a
COME ON, like he hadn't finished puberty.   Irritating, yes,
but the fact I lost the two breakers, mentally and physically
I could not fight anymore. And I always thought I could
fight in a match forever.   But Lleyton breaks your will. He
loves that part and you can see it in his eyes. And what's

even worse is that off the court he is a nice 'bro' type guy. A guy you would want to shoot the ---- with and have a beer. But he won't - and I suspect only because he doesn't want to give up his edge... 'The Mongoose' never lets go..."

Hewitt leads series 1-0

2000   French Open   R128   Hewitt 76 76 63

"I always loved to watch him play."

Richard Krajicek: "I think I played him at Stuttgart indoors. And I lost. I don't remember much. I remember watching him play. Great competitor. I really thought he was a good guy, on and off the court. And I always loved to watch him play. And actually, every time, even now, like when he came back from 5-love down at the French Open in the fifth set, it was great. Unfortunately he did not win that match (vs. Gilles Simon). Even now he's older, he's still a great competitor."

Question: What do you remember about your match with him?

Richard Krajicek: "To be honest, I don't even remember anything about it. It was an interview - he was playing at the tournament that I'm tournament director of now (Rotterdam - ABN AMRO World Tenins Tournament, an ATP World Tour 500 event) - somebody asked him if we played. He said, Yeah we played once. That's how I know that we played each other [smiles]. I mean, I totally blacked that match out. Most of the matches I lost I black out, so [smiles]. So I really don't remember and I can't tell you anything about how it is to play him. I just don't remember. I just know I lost. One thing I can say about Hewitt is that with some players, once you got on top of them, you had a good chance of winning. With Hewitt, you really had to win the last point to make sure that you won."

Hewitt leads series   1-0

2000   Stuttgart   R32   Hewitt   64 75

"It's like to play a computer."

Dudi Sela: "[Laughs] They were very tough matches with Hewitt. We fought for every point, every ball. Also, the first time I played him it was a lot of pressure. He was number one in the world, there is an aura behind him. But second time, for me, was much better. But I think he is one of the toughest pros to play, fighting for every point. Great player, great attitude. And he is a nice guy outside the court, on the court."

Question: Did you become friends, practice together?

Dudi Sela: "Not much but he always says hello. I practice with him two times."

Question: Was there anything surprising about playing him?

Dudi Sela: "No [chuckles]. You know what you're gonna

get every match."

Question: Enjoyable to play Hewitt or is it too grueling?

Dudi Sela: "Every point, a lot of balls back. He's doing the same thing every point. It's like to play a computer."

Question: Pleased with your second performance against him? I remember being there seeing it in Washington DC, it was a close match.

Dudi Sela: "Yes. Yes. I don't really remember it, to tell you the truth. I don't really remember. It was a long time ago. I think it was a close match. He played well."

Hewitt leads series 4-0

```
2008   Adelaide   R32   Hewitt 62 62
2009   Miami Masters R128   Hewitt 36 64 63
2009   Washington DC   R32   Hewitt 63 26 62
2012   Newport   QF   Hewitt 64 63
```

"Unbelievable fighter."

Thiemo de Bakker: "He's like a wall. Doesn't miss. Unbelievable fighter. And great mentality."

Question: How did you fare in your matches with Hewitt?

Thiemo de Bakker: "Lost both."

Question: Pleased with your performances?

Thiemo de Bakker: "Yes and no. I was still young. One time I played okay, the other time I had no chance. So, okay."

Question: Did anything surprise you about Hewitt?

Thiemo de Bakker: "No. I mean, he's a wall. Competing really well and he's behind every shot and that makes it tough."

Hewitt leads series 2-0

2009   Munich R16   Hewitt 63 64
2009   Halle R16   Hewitt 63 63

"I love to watch him."

Stanislas Wawrinka: "I love to play him. I think he's a great competitor. He was number one, he was an amazing player. Still an amazing fighter. He always fights, always gives everything. Even when I lose to him I think it's always a good match. I like the feeling that you play a guy that will give you everything because I try to do more of the same with my game. With every match we fight for every ball. It's always a great match to play him. And I love to watch him."

Hewitt vs. Wawrinka series tied 2-2

2007   Cincinnati Masters   R64   Hewitt 75 36 76
2011   Davis Cup Playoff RR   Wawrinka 46 64 67 64 63
2013   Indian Wells Masters   R32   Wawrinka 64 75
2013   Wimbledon R128   Hewitt 64 75 63

"His game suits my game."

Ivo Karlovic: "The feeling of playing Hewitt, is if you win it's good, if you lose it's bad [smiles]. But I can say I have positive scores so I like it against him."

Question: Is he difficult or unique to play against?

Ivo Karlovic: "He's unbelievably tough because his legs are unbelievable, his footwork. I don't know. I like to play him. His game suits my game. I believe so."

Karlovic leads series 4-1

2003   Wimbledon   R128   Karlovic   16 76 63 64
2005   Queens Club   QF   Karlovic   76 63
2007   Tokyo   QF   Karlovic   76 76
2009   French Open   R 128   Hewitt 67 67 76 64 63
2012   Queens Club   R64 Karlovic   63 62

"He did things that aren't possible."

Greg Rusedski: "My first memory of Hewitt was in Adelaide when he beat Andre Agassi in the semifinal. Then I saw him the week after in Australia. But he's always been a guy that if you had to have someone play for your life, he's the guy you'd want to play. Kind of reminiscent of the Jimmy Connors of old. A guy who maximized everything he possibly can and just loves the game and wants to keep on competing no matter what. He's a walking miracle right now with that toe surgery and all the surgeries he's had, to be playing the way that he is. He absolutely loves the game."

Question: What was your most memorable match with Hewitt?

Greg Rusedski: "Probably the ones that I won. I beat him in Indianapolis one year. I lost to him a few times at Queens Club. But we always had really close, tight matches against Lleyton. He's just a great competitor and someone who always wants to win."

Question: Can you share an on or off court anecdote that captures Hewitt's essence?

Greg Rusedski: "[Laughs] Let me see...that captures his essence...Probably all of those shouts of 'COME ON' every two seconds is the essence of him and then copying that thing that Mats Wilander used to do, his fist pump at winning those matches. But I just think the essence of Hewitt is just winning matches that he shouldn't win. Just doing things that aren't possible. Basically, between Sampras and Federer's domination, he was the man in the middle who really got the number one and then maximized everything he could. So it just shows you what sheer determination and desire can do."

Hewitt leads series 4-3

```
1999   Nottingham   QF   Rusedski   64 75
2000   Basel    QF   Hewitt   76 62
2000   Stuttgart   QF   Hewitt 64 64
2001   San Jose   QF   Rusedski   57 61   64
2001   Queens Club    QF    Hewitt   64 64
2002   Indianapolis   R16    Rusedski   76 64

2005   Cincinnati Masters   R32   Hewitt   16 75 64
```

"It just blew my mind."

Taylor Dent: "I saw him in the juniors. We grew up playing in the juniors. My first memory is kind of out of nowhere. He was always a good junior player but out of nowhere he got a wildcard into Adelaide and he ended up winning the thing. And he beat a lot of good players on the way to the title. It just blew my mind."

Question: He beat Agassi and Stoltenberg.

Taylor Dent: "Yeah. At the time it was an unbelievable win."

Question: Describe what it was like to play him?

Taylor Dent: "It was tough for me. It was a disaster of a match up. I played him a lot of times. I only ever got him once. Actually in his hometown of Adelaide. And he was just tough. I liked attacking. And he was very accurate with his shots. He was able to dip it down at my feet. When I came to the net, he was able to lob it over my head. It posed a lot of problems for my style of game."

Question: You must have played incredibly well the day you beat him?

Taylor Dent: "You know what? It's interesting. The courts were quick and I kind of changed the tactics a little bit. I ended up staying back at the baseline and just kind of chipping and waiting for a golden opportunity to come in. And he was a little bit off. He didn't pass quite as well as normal. And that's kind of the way how it goes."

Question: Do you have a memory or anecdote that captures Hewitt's essence, on or off court?

Taylor Dent: "Off court, for me, he was always great. There was the stage when I was - I was getting good enough coming up to where I was being considered for Davis Cup. And so obviously with my background - my dad's Australian - he gave me a call up to try and lobby for me to come play for the Australian team. And he was very nice on the phone and that's kind of how he was. A good guy, a straight-forward guy. He doesn't really beat-around-the-bush too much and I appreciate that."

Hewitt leads series   5-1

2001   Wimbledon   R64   Hewitt   16 75 63 67 63
2001   Indianapolis   R32   Hewitt 62 76
2003   Scottsdale   SF   Hewitt 62 64
2005   Adelaide   QF   Dent 76 63
2005   Wimbledon   R16   Hewitt 64 64 67 63
2005   US Open   R32   Hewitt 63 36 67 62 75

"I expected to steamroll the kid."

Vince Spadea: "I played against Hewitt in the 1998 quarters at Adelaide, his hometown in the south of Australia, when he was a sixteen year old wildcard. Everyone was wondering how he got a wildcard in the first place, because he was like No. 500 in the world at the time and nobody had ever heard of him. Some of the other Australian players were mystified. He had just played a Satellite, which is an even lower pro tournament than a

Challenger, that has since been mostly phased out in favor of Futures, the week before Adelaide, and he had lost to a nobody. Our match was a night match, center court. I see this little guy with long blond hair who looks like a surfer, walk out on the court. I figure: 'I'm in the semis. This kid is sixteen and he looked weak, inexperienced, unrehearsed, and unpolished.'"

"The match begins and he's holding his own. He keeps on hitting balls in the court. I wasn't playing strongly enough or consistently enough to overpower him even though I've got him outweighed by about forty pounds. I end up losing the first set 7-5. Now I'm thinking: 'What does this kid think he's doing?' He didn't miss one shot long the entire set. My dad, who was coaching me, said after the match, 'He missed into the net and he missed wide but he never missed past the baseline.' Whenever Hewitt won a big point he screeched out, 'COME ON' and punched the air with his fist. I thought that was a little annoying and cocky of him but I didn't let it bother or intimidate me. I won the second set 6-3. I had been working with Jim Pierce (coach and father of Mary Pierce), so I was in great shape. I had been killing myself in training. I expected to steamroll the kid in the third set. But instead, he put his game into another gear and beat me soundly 6-1 to win the match."

"The next day I was sitting eating breakfast with my dad in the player's cafeteria and Brad Gilbert, coach of Andre Agassi, walked up to us and completely ignored me. He approached my dad and said, 'Your son had Hewitt last night but he choked. Andre will show you how to handle the kid tonight.'"

"Of course, Hewitt straight-setted Agassi 76 76 and then went on to win the tournament. Hewitt has gone on to win almost twenty million dollars in his career, along with a

Wimbledon and U.S. Open title. He's a true warrior on the court. He doesn't get fazed by disappointment or failure. He doesn't worry about if he's hitting the ball great or if he's winning or losing, he just enjoys the battle. The only other player who battled as successfully as Hewitt was Jimmy Connors. Hewitt will never give up and he doesn't mind if he has to win hard or easy. He's one of the greatest competitors in tennis."

Hewitt leads series 7-0

```
1998    Adelaide   QF   Hewitt   75 36 61
1999    Lyon     SF    Hewitt   63 63
2003    Indian Wells Masters   Hewitt 75 61
2006    Sydney   R32    Hewitt   26 75 63
2006    San Jose   SF   Hewitt 63 64
2006    Washington DC   Hewitt    R32 67 76 64
2007    Las Vegas   RR   Hewitt   63 63
```

"I don't remember if I beat him."

Nikolay Davydenko: "He was very difficult to play. I played him a few times. I don't even remember if I beat him. I know he beat me a few times. We are about the same age but he came on the Tour much earlier than I did. He came on as a big player in 2000-2001. I start to have my best years on the Tour in 2005."

Question: What was your most memorable match with Hewitt?

Nikolay Davydenko: "He was very hard to play. I remember we had a tough match in Hamburg. He won 6-4 in the third. We also had a good match at French Open. He won in four sets but it was a good match. I enjoy to play with Hewitt."

Hewitt leads series 4-0

2001   French Open R64   Hewitt 60 61 63

2003 French Open R64   Hewitt 63 46 63 76

2005 Cincinnati Masters QF Hewitt 62 63

2007 Hamburg   Masters R16   Hewitt   64 26 64

"He can pass you from any shot."

Jan Hernych: "It's always very difficult to play against him because he's a great player and very experienced. And also he's one of the greatest fighters. He never gives up, even if he's down. It's one of the most difficult guys to play on the Tour, yeah."

Question: What is your most memorable match against Hewitt?

Jan Hernych: "I think I had the first chance to beat him at Wimbledon. I lost 3-1. I think I had the chance in the second set to finish the set for my side but. Yeah, I think Wimbledon was the closest one for me."

Question: What surprised you about playing Hewitt?

Jan Hernych: "Well, the first time he was serving very well. It was a surprise for me because I didn't expect that good of serving from him. That was the biggest surprise. I know he's a fighter, he can run very fast. And he can pass you from any point on the court. But the biggest surprise was how he served."

Question: Is it enjoyable to play Hewitt? Or is it frustrating because you know it's going to be such a struggle?

Jan Hernych: "It's always hard matches. It's not enjoyable because my game is trying to attack the opponent and trying, going for volleys. And with Lleyton, you never know, even with a difficult ball he can pass you from any shot. It's more difficult to play him than enjoyable."

Question: I saw the match you almost had him in Newport this year, it went three sets. What happened?

Jan Hernych: "Yeah. I had a chance in Newport, I just lost a bad game at the start of the second set. And then we were fighting for one game in the second set, 3-all or something, I'm not sure of the score, then I lost my serve and he was just better on the court after this. But I also have a chance with him in Newport but in Grand Slams it's always more important to beat this guy."

Question: Have you had any interaction with him off court?

Jan Hernych: "Not really. Not really. No we are not...even if we played a lot of times (seven) we don't...we're not very close. He doesn't have any friendly relations."

Hewitt leads series 7-0

2005   Wimbledon   R64   Hewitt   62 75 36 63

2006   Adelaide   R32 Hewitt   46 62 64

2006   Las Vegas   R16   Hewitt   63 63

2006   French Open R128   Hewitt   76 36 62 60

2006   U.S. Open   R64   Hewitt   64 62 62

2009   Indian Wells Masters   R128   Hewitt 76 63

2013   Newport   QF   Hewitt 67 64 62

"He was a lion on the court."

Davide Sanguinetti: "I played him when he was number in the world. He was the best. I remember once in Cincinnati and I retired. Because my daughter was gonna be born so I had to leave. So I found an excuse and I run away with it. But I don't think I had a chance with him that day [smiles]."

Question: What was it like to play Hewitt at his best (in previous round of Cincinnati match with Sanguinetti, Hewitt beat Robby Ginepri 6-0 6-0)?

Davide Sanguinetti: "I think it was tough to make a point because he was such a fighter on the court, which he still is, but before he could run a little faster than now. And to make a point you had to sweat because of the pain."

Question: Stand out memory of Hewitt?

Davide Sanguinetti: "He was all around. You cannot say

he had like unbelievable forehand, backhand, but he was an all around player. That he put all his heart out on the court. He was a lion on the court."

Question: Did you look forward to playing him? Or was it like, Oh God, this guy is so hard to play?

Davide Sanguinetti: "He was so hard to play. But I always enjoyed to play with the top players. So I always wanted to play with the top players."

Hewitt leads series 2-0

2001 'S-Hertogenbosch R32 Hewitt 62 61

2002 Cincinnati Masters R32 Hewitt 50 (ret.)

"It was a turning point in the history of tennis."

Ivan Ljubicic: "When I played Hewitt he had just won Wimbledon. He was at the top of his game. I remember that I qualified and I think it was quarterfinals so for me it was a great week anyway. And it was 7-6 6-7 and he ended up winning 6-4. I was 5-1 down and I came back to 5-4 and he won it. But it's incredible that we played only once and we were around together on the Tour maybe fifteen years. And not ever close - I can't remember like even being close to playing him. So it's unbelievable. But obviously he is a great fighter and I think the way he managed his career - we would love that he played more. For so many years after

U.S. Open he would take a break and prepare for Australian Open. I feel like, with all the injuries that he had, and he had many, the type of game that he played, he managed his tennis incredibly well. To be able to be still on the Tour at 33 and still fighting and playing at this level."

Question: Did anything surprise you about him?

Ivan Ljubicic: "No, not really. The thing is that he's an unbelievable fighter. But what I say - it doesn't mean he's only saying 'COME ON' - he finds the way to win matches. He's always very, very difficult to play. Obviously, with now, it's different than it was ten years ago. But to win Wimbledon, to win U.S. Open with the game that he had, back then, it was a turning point in the history of tennis. Because he was the first one really to win Wimbledon from the baseline, like playing this way, not like Agassi, because he was still hitting the balls. He was the first one to really, like, demolish Sampras' serve in the final of U.S. Open. So he is, let's say, the first one of this new generation of really, really solid players."

Question: Did you get along well with Hewitt off court? Ever practice together?

Ivan Ljubicic: "We practiced a few times. He's really shy, actually, you know, incredibly. Off the court he's kind of calm, doesn't really talk to anybody, really shy.   We obviously, being of similar age, we got along because we spent so much time together on the Tour. So I like him a lot, actually."

Hewitt leads head to head 1-0

2001   Cincinnati Masters   QF   Hewitt 76 67 64

"Marcelo Rios told me Hewitt was going to be No. 1."

Guillermo Canas: "I have a lot of memories of playing Hewitt. I played many times against him. I remember once when he was really young we met in Delray Beach, Florida. I think the first time we played was in qualies of one tournament. He beat me. And then I beat him in Houston, I think in '99. I think the first time I make a final in ATP was against him. I lost in the final to him in 'S-Hertogenbosch. I beat him in round 16 in Roland Garros once and I lost once in five sets. But my memories...it was always really tough fighting when we play each other. It was long matches. I think he's one of the greatest competitors of this sport."

Question: Did you enjoy to play Hewitt?

Guillermo Canas: "I loved to play him. I know what I have in front of me, is a guy who is going to fight for every point, like me. And always we were at certain sides of the court a lot and always we have really tough matches."

Question: Any interaction with Hewitt off court? Ever practice together?

Guillermo Canas: "We practice some. But we don't have a relationship, like two guys who played the Tour for many years. I know him, I say Hi all the time. He travels the last years with a guy I know really well."

Question: Did anything surprise you about Hewitt?

Guillermo Canas: "I'm not surprised. I know him when he

was fifteen, watching on TV he won his first ATP title in his hometown. And I know he's going to be a really good player. Every year he surprises me more and more, when he got to number one in the world and some moments. It was really, really tough to beat him on any courts. But I have one memory when he was so young. I practice with Marcelo Rios. At that moment Rios was number one or number two in the world. And he told me, 'That guy is gonna be the next number one.' Eventhough he was in the forties in the rankings. It was funny. I said, 'No way.' And Rios was right. He told me he was going to be number one. He was right."

Hewitt leads head to head 6-2

1999   Orlando   R16   Canas   63 63

1999   Delray Beach   R32   Hewitt 67 (12) 62 64

1999   Nottingham   R16   Hewitt 62 75

2001   French Open R16   Hewitt 36 67 62 63 63

2001   'S-Hertogenbosch   F   Hewitt 63 64

2001   Stuttgart   R16 Hewitt   36 61 64

2002   French Open R16 Canas   67 (1)76 (13) 64 63

2007   Wimbledon   R32 Hewitt 64 36 63 64

"It's a real honor to play that guy."

Ruben Bemelmans: "I played him twice, in Davis Cup

and Hopman Cup. Playing Lleyton is always a special feeling because he's a former number one. He's one of the legends of tennis. And to play him it's unbelievable steadiness in his game. So it's very difficult to make points against him. It's one of the matches I will always remember."

Question: Were you pleased with your performance?

Ruben Bemelmans: "Yeah. Very much. I played against him twice. I lost twice. But every time it was a battle. It was a close match. Even in Davis Cup I had the feeling I was a little better at a certain point. Like I told you, he's so experienced that he has an answer for every ball, every time, whenever. It was really nice to play against him."

Question: Did anything surprise you about him?

Ruben Bemelmans: "Not really. From the first point, he's there. He's not waiting for anything. He's right there, right in the match from the first points. As you see, from some other players, they take it easy from the beginning to see how the other one is playing. But Lleyton tries [smiles] the famous COME ONS - he did already in the first game. From that I was a little surprised. But the rest, I knew how he played before. I knew what I was up against."

Question: What were you able to do tactics-wise that was effective against Hewitt?

Ruben Bemelmans: "He likes to play counter. He has a very good passing shot. He reads the game really well. Against Lleyton, it's important to put him under pressure. And maybe it's risky business but I think you have to play like this against him. Because if you go from the baseline and you play the rallies, he's not going to miss. So you have to take some risks at a certain point. And if you feel well then I think there's no problem. But he can make you doubt. I think that's his strength as well. But you've got to play aggressive and go for the points."

Question: Is it enjoyable to play him? Or is it too much of a grueling grind?

Ruben Bemelmans: "A bit both. When you're playing, it's tough. Then you remember who you're playing against and then it's fun again [smiles]. But I think he will always stay tough on the court. He's a fighter. Those kinds of players are tough to play against. It's a real honor to play that guy."

Question: Did you have any interactions with him off court? Ever practice together?

Ruben Bemelmans: "Not really, no. When we pass each other we say Hi. But never have a conversation with him. How he is I cannot say."

Question: Did Hewitt use any intimidation tactics before the match? Like Jan-Michael Gambill once told me Marcelo Rios tried to stare him down in the player's lounge before their match.

Ruben Bemelmans: "No [laughs]. I think he will not be impressed by the thing I'll be doing. No. I just went on court with my tactics, gameplan, and just did my thing."

Hewitt leads series 2-0

2010 Davis Cup   Hewitt   76 75 26 64

2011 Hopman Cup (exhibition)   Hewitt   64 63

"We played Hewitt and Rafael Nadal in Montreal."

Pierre-Ludovic Duclos: "I played him in doubles. I played him in 2008 at the Rogers Cup in Montreal. I didn't get a wildcard in singles but I got a wildcard in doubles. It was me and Philip Bester. We played Hewitt and Rafael Nadal. They were actually playing together."

Question: Describe the feeling of walking on the court as a youngster going out to play Rafael Nadal and Lleyton Hewitt?

Pierre-Ludovic Duclos: "It was a little intimidating to play those two big-name players but at the same time I felt it was a great experience and opportunity. I definitely felt nervous at the start of the match. I think the biggest obstacle is the mental issue when you plays guys like Hewitt and Nadal. To see yourself winning the match at the end of the day is very hard. If you can overcome those thoughts it's half the battle."

Question: Memories of the match?

Pierre-Ludovic Duclos: "What I remember is Hewitt is a player that doesn't have much power but he has such good timing and hand-eye coordination. He uses your power against you. Especially on the return of serve his timing is amazing, also from the baseline. He hits the ball flat, he doesn't use much top spin. His timing and hand-eye coordination are what stood out for me. They won the match. We lost 6-4 6-4. I remember we were up in the first set, we were up a break. The second set was the same thing, we were ahead 4-1 and we lost again, same thing. I was nineteen, Bester was seventeen or eighteen then. I remember Hewitt came up with some really good passing shots on crucial points. After the match we exchanged some words, that was it. We shook hands at the net and he said to me, 'Good match, Keep on doing the hard work, you have good potential.'"

"What an incredible competitor."

Michael Joyce: "When I played Hewitt I'm pretty sure he was top five at the time. It was my second to last tournament, before I retired. I had just beaten Jan-Michael Gambill, which was a pretty good win at the time he was top twenty. A couple of things stood out to me about the match with Hewitt. We played a night match basically in my back yard at UCLA, sold-out crowd all in my favor. What surprised me was how well Hewitt served. He was placing his serve on a dime at the time. I think that's something he hasn't done as well in the last six or seven years. Also, funny story happened during the match. I was playing him close, it was four-all or five-all first set and he was serving. I won a great point at deuce and the crowd went nuts. So right before breakpoint after the crowd simmered down, my buddy who was drunk at the time stood up and yelled, 'Hey Hewitt, Joyce is going to break you, he's gonna BREAK YOU!!' The whole crowd heard it and started laughing. Hewitt won the next point, fist-pumped my friend and stepped it up a level and I didn't win another game the rest of the match [smiles]. I saw my friend after the match and he said that probably wasn't a good idea. What an incredible competitor Hewitt is."

Hewitt leads series 1-0

2003   Los Angeles   R32   Hewitt 63 60

"To win against him you have to give everything."

Nenad Zimonjic: "I played him once in singles. A couple of times in doubles. I have to say he is an unbelievable competitor, always fighting, tries his best. To win against him you have to give everything. He's a great champion. He's always there to support his country to play Davis Cup which is a big history for all the Aussie guys. I think he's one of the last guys who is thinking about representing his country and playing Davis Cup matches."

Question: What is your most memorable match with Hewitt?

Nenad Zimonjic: "I just played once in the qualifying match in singles in Scottsdale. It was way back. I can't remember which year. There were a couple of doubles matches that I played against him. Once in the finals of Barcelona. He was playing with Mark Knowles, I was playing with Daniel Nestor. We were fortunate to win. I lost to him at Wimbledon, close sets last year (2012). So it was interesting to have him on the other side of the court, with one of the best returners of all time. It's always good for somebody with my style of game - server and volleyer - to have somebody who is the best at what he does, which is returns, passing shots, lobs and a great competitor."

"He was always very pumped when he was playing."

Kenneth Carlsen: "I remember I played him when he was playing really well. I just remember that he was running really, really well. He got every ball back. You have to win every single point which was tough because he ran everything down. I was trying to play aggressive but he just got everything back. He put a lot of pressure on the opponents the way that he played. Which is...you feel like you have to win every point. And if you didn't play very, very sharp, he was going to punish you. At the same time, if he had a short ball, he was not afraid of coming in and taking advantage of that one. So he was like playing against a wall and everything just came back."

Question: You played Hewitt once?

Kenneth Carlsen: "We played a couple of times. Two or three. I just now remember, fast, the last two."

Question: What was your most memorable match with Hewitt?

Kenneth Carlsen: "Actually, I didn't play well against him because he was a bad match up for me. First time, actually, I was injured. That was not memorable for me because I couldn't serve and without a serve it was tough for me against him. The second time he played well. It was tough for me to play against a guy like him. When he was at his best he was fighting and got everything back. And when I came to the net he was just passing me. Getting all my serves back, returning well. Just an unbelievably solid player."

Question: Lasting memory of Hewitt?

Kenneth Carlsen: "I always had a good relationship with him. He was always very pumped when he was playing. But I never had a problem with that. He just wanted to win and he was very focused and mentally tough. In my opinion, I had a good relation with him."

Hewitt leads series 3-0

1999 Singapore   R16   Hewitt   61 62
2003 Los Angeles   QF   Hewitt   67 64 63
2004 Washington DC R32   Hewitt   61 62

"He's just a beast out there. I would compare Hewitt to a boxer."

Jan-Michael Gambill: "We played seven times and Hewitt was one of the toughest competitors on the court. I actually really enjoyed all the matches we played. They were always close. Whether he won or I won, it was a battle. He's just a beast out there. He didn't have the biggest strokes, he didn't have the biggest serve but he was one of the few guys who could match me for intensity, and that's saying something. Because I played with almost unmatched intensity, I thought, when I was playing well. I was always kind of in the heat of the battle. I loved it. I relished the battle more than I loved playing tennis. I don't know Hewitt well enough to say that about him but judging from our matches I would think he was very similar, he loves to fight. He makes tennis more like boxing.   Which is kind of how I do things. That was the analogy my dad always threw in my face - it's a lot like boxing. I argued that for years but then I finally came to agree with him. So I would compare Hewitt to a boxer."

Question: What was your most memorable match with Hewitt?

Jan-Michael Gambill: "I have two. I played some really good matches against him. The ones that I won were hugely memorable for me. I beat him first round at Wimbledon. That was the year that I made quarterfinals. Beat him badly that time. Quickest of the matches that we played."

Question: What happened there?

Jan-Michael Gambill: "I went out with a gameplan and I stuck to it. I just had a great day. I had a great day. Maybe he was off that day, I don't know. The days that I was able to keep my error ratio low and serve well - I was in command of those matches and those were the ones that I won. When he got kind of inside my head a bit and made me start making some errors, were the ones that I lost. It was, like a lot of my matches that I played, I'm the bigger hitter than most of these guys. It was kind of in my control. And then he could get under my skin, which he was able to do the four times he beat me it went his way, I made too many errors. So that day I didn't make a lot of errors at Wimbledon."

"The first time we played was in Scottsdale when I won my very first ATP tournament. I'd beaten Sampras and Agassi that tournament. So beating those three guys in any event - not a lot of guys have done that. So that's super memorable for me as well. And then Miami. I played him in the semifinals of Miami. And won that one. I believe that was three sets. And then I lost to Andre in the finals. So those are three very memorable matches - winning a tournament, making quarterfinals of a slam, making the finals of the fifth-largest tournament in the world. Was all very memorable for me. So they were actually huge points of my career. Then he beat me in a bunch of different places as well. I can't remember those quite as much [laughs]. But I really enjoyed playing against Lleyton. We always had kind of a mutual respect for each other. I respected him quite a bit on and off the court. We were never friends but we were always friendly. And good for him, he's had a great career."

Question: Did anything surprise you about him?

Jan-Michael Gambill: "I don't think anything really surprised me about him. With Lleyton Hewitt you know what you're gonna get. It's like going out on the court with Connors. He wasn't quite Connors but he was damn near close. He was that kind of player. He's never gonna give up, he's never gonna give you an inch. And that's awesome. I think he's made the most of his career. A little jealous that he's been able to play longer than me, with my injuries. Besides that, more power to him, he's had a very good career."

Question: What is your very first memory of Hewitt?

Jan-Michael Gambill: "Was seeing him in Scottsdale and thinking: 'That guy's gonna get to the finals.' And I think he had to beat Rafter that week. He had to have a couple of really big wins on his side of the draw. And I had goliaths in front of me, of American tennis, and legends of the game. But seeing him - thinking: 'That's a feisty son-of-a-bitch. I think he's gonna be in the finals. And I think he's gonna be a great player.'"

Question: Can you share a memory or anecdote of Hewitt off court? Did you practice together?

Jan-Michael Gambill: "Lleyton and I practiced plenty. He's one of those guys that took the same ethic as I did. Practice like you play. So the same type of battles would happen on the practice court. We didn't practice all that much but here and there. And they were always high-intensity, the kind of practices that I looked for."

Hewitt leads series   4-3

1999   Scottsdale   F   Gambill   76 46 64
2000   Miami Masters   QF   Hewitt   64 76
2000   Wimbledon   R128   Gambill   63 62 75
2001   Miami Masters   SF   Gambill 75 64
2002   San Jose   SF Hewitt   75 64
2002   Indian Wells Masters   R16   Hewitt   62 64
2002   Miami Masters   R32   Hewitt   36 64 75

"He was 'The Nadal' of that era."

Jeff Coetzee: "I remember meeting him the first time at the John Newcombe/Owen Davidson Tennis Academy.You could tell this kid was gonna be good. I knew he was something special. When we first met he was about fourteen and I was eighteen. There was already big talk about Hewitt at Newk's and since I was the number one there, we had to play a practice set. So I can say I beat him in a practice set [smiles]. But I already knew then that he was gonna be extra special. He was different at Newk's as a fourteen year old,   how he had an understanding of the game and he knew exactly what he wanted. I think two years after that he won the ATP title in Adelaide at age sixteen, if I remember correctly."

"I was lucky enough to play him at the Stockholm Open in 2002 in doubles where he partnered with Joachim Pim Pim Johansson. He was number one in the world at that time. The reception that he could inspire was unreal and I'll never forget what a great atmosphere it was playing him. He always has a 'never give up' attitude and you always knew even if you are a break up it's never over with Hewitt. It's never over. I just love his ability to get in people's minds. I felt all the players thought they needed to do something extra to beat him and they would get outside their comfort zone. He was 'The Nadal' from that era."

"He did not show very good sportsmanship."

Jimmy Wang: "When I played vs Hewitt it was during the Davis Cup and doubles match. In 2008 in Chinese Taipei. It was a five set match. Personally I don't know him as person. And I don't really like him as a person or as a player. He was arrogant and in my opinion he did not show very good sportsmanship on the court."

Question: Who were the other two players on court? Was Hewitt shouting his signature Come Ons?

Jimmy Wang: "He was playing with Paul Hanley and I play with Yen-Hsun Lu. I'm not sure exactly what he was saying on the court."

2008   Davis Cup RR   Hanley/Hewitt   62 76 46 26 26

"He was like a magnet."

Justin Gimelstob: "I played him a bunch of times. The first time was in Washington DC, Asia, Center Court at Wimbledon and Bangkok, Thailand. Four times.   The first time we played he was really young. We played in Washington that summer - the same year he beat Agassi in Adelaide and won the title (as an unknown wildcard '98). I beat him in three sets. The same year I lost to him in Singapore 7-6 in the third. The next time it was seven years later at Wimbledon on Center Court he won in three tough sets. The last match was in Bangkok, I lost 7-6 in the third."

Question: Your impressions of playing Hewitt those four times?

Justin Gimelstob: "He didn't change much throughout his career. He was always an incredible competitor. He was always an incredible defender. Underrated serve, good location. Very good at net, good hands. Brutal with a target on his passing shots. One of the best returners of serve in the sport. For a two year period he was utterly dominant. I always respected his amazing commitment to Davis Cup, his commitment to excellence. Lleyton Hewitt is just a warrior. He was one of those guys who really maximized his talent."

Question: Your results with Hewitt show four close, hard-fought matches. Did your style match up well with his?

Justin Gimelstob: "I played a few decent matches against him at different stages of his career. The first two he was very young. He beat me at Wimbledon on Center Court - I did play well there. The last match he was still ranked pretty high - I played well there also. He won three of the four matches."

Question: Do you remember what your strategy/tactics were that worked well against Hewitt? What you were able to do that gave him problems?

Justin Gimelstob: "Because Hewitt is such a good returner, you have to be very conscious of mixing up your serve speeds and locations. You need to use the body serve and mix up when you serve and volley because he is so skilled with a target. Also, I tried to put pressure on his second serve. Hewitt also has one of the best and most consistent cross court backhands so I tried to keep him out of that pattern by using my backhand down the line. In addition, while Hewitt is one of the best absorbers of pace, he isn't as impressive at creating pace. Thus, I believe a good strategy against Hewitt is to make him create his own pace and challenge him to be the aggressor at times. Also, at times, Hewitt had the tendency to block back his forehand return, when he was doing that I would serve and volley more to that side."

Question: How are/were your interactions with Hewitt off court?

Justin Gimelstob: "He was always very respectful. He's a good guy. In the later years of his career, he's traveled with his wife and kids. I've spent time playing with his kids. It helps that his wife is very sweet. It's a different dynamic with having your kids around. It helps that I also have a good relationship with his coach Peter Luczak."

Question: Did anything surprise you about Hewitt?

Justin Gimelstob: "No. He's pretty much what you see: A great champion, a great competitor. During those two years when he was dominant, you just couldn't get the ball away from him. He was like a magnet. He moved so incredibly well. Novak Djokovic and Andy Murray play somewhat similar styles but they can hit the ball harder so they can create more. For two years Hewitt was utterly dominant, especially on hard courts."

Question: Pound for pound, do you think Hewitt is one of the best ever?

Justin Gimelstob: "Pound for pound, for sure. What he got out of his game, the success he's had - for sure."

Hewitt leads series 3-1

1998	Washington DC	R64	Gimelstob	63 26 62
1998	Singapore	R16	Hewitt	67 62 76
2005	Wimbledon	R32	Hewitt 76 64 75
2005	Bangkok	R16	Hewitt 64 57 76 (9)

"I was never close to beating him."

Stefan Koubek: "Well, it was always very hard to play

him. Unfortunately, I was never close to beating him but on the court it felt like he was not doing too much but he did not miss and he always made you play. He was the kind of player you had to beat with great tennis. There was no easy points and he moved unbelievably well. When you thought you had him he came up with some ridiculous shots! Big respect for Lleyton Hewitt!"

Hewitt leads series 3-0

1999	Delray Beach	R16	Hewitt 26 63 64
2000	Rome Masters	R64	Hewitt 64 62
2000	Indianapolis	R32	Hewitt 61 60

"Hewitt most definitely has a soul to him."

Geoff Grant: "The lucky thing for me is I got Hewitt in the early part of his career. So at that time I kind of knew that I was beating a good player. But I had the fortune that I was playing great, great tennis. I ended up winning the tournament (Winnetka Challenger in '98) after I beat him. And probably because I beat him I ended up winning the tournament, because it gave me the confidence. But I was fortunate to get him when he was still coming up. He wasn't even in the top hundred at the time. And it made a big difference in the match because I wasn't intimidated by him because he was still this young kid, seventeen years old. Yeah, he had beaten Agassi in the semifinals of

Adelaide...that was just a huge advantage for me and I happened to take advantage of it when I beat Lleyton."

Question: What is your first memory of Lleyton Hewitt?

Geoff Grant: "A talented kid out of nowhere. Because he was coming from Down Under. At that time you didn't expect any superstars coming out of Australia. And he just exploded on the scene. He was this young, talented kid. Basically, the next generation arrived when Hewitt won that tournament in Adelaide."

Question: For your match with Hewitt, describe the scene, how many fans were watching, day or night match?

Geoff Grant: "It was great for me, there was only about a hundred fifty people watching, a hundred people. It was a small tournament in Winnetka, Illinois. It was in August just before the U.S. Open. It was a day match on center court. They had built a small stadium. Actually, people came out to watch him because he had arrived on the scene. He was a phenom that we hadn't seen in a long time. Since those guys like Agassi, Sampras, Chang who came up at a very young age. So Hewitt was noteworthy and everyone was paying attention to him."

Question: Your memories of this match?

Geoff Grant: "I remember starting out great and I broke him in the fourth game, I believe, of the first set. And so, again, that helped me break down this barrier of, like, this guy had beaten Agassi but he's still this young kid and he's still not top hundred. So I wasn't intimidated. So I broke him. And he ended up breaking back. And then I had to think about it. And then I just played a great game. Because my return was my great weapon. And his serve wasn't huge, especially at that time. He hadn't developed a big serve yet and he certainly couldn't hit the spots. So I was able to keep taking advantage of his serve and finally I broke him at 5-all. And then held for the set."

"And then after that I don't remember much other than a break of serve. There wasn't anything really noteworthy, 5 and 3. He was gracious. He definitely was mature beyond his years at that time. I think he recognized that he was probably going to do some special things in the sport so he kind of accepted it. He's always been nice to me. When I would see him he would be respectful too."

Question: Was Hewitt's famous intensity on the court evident in your match?

Geoff Grant: "It's tough because I had won the match 5 and 3. The memory was on that day it was intense but it was a perfect match up for me. At that time, he hadn't developed his weapons big enough. The court was fairly fast. It was a hard court and I was serving very well. And I was able to dictate play because I played with two hands on each side - I'm taking balls early - and he likes a rhythm, he likes to kind of grind the point out. I was taking balls early and taking away his speed in a way, in trying to re-direct him. So it's kind of strange, I don't remember the intensity at that time. It was a one-sided match after the first set. But it wasn't a walkover either."

Question: Were you surprised at his later success - two Grand Slam major titles, two year-ends ranked number one in the world?

Geoff Grant: "I was not surprised. Because I knew that I had had a huge win when I beat him. Because I won that tournament. It was one of those weeks that you hope to have as an athlete. And that was my week. I didn't have the pressure of being on a Grand Slam stage at the U.S. Open, on Louis Armstrong Stadium, of having to play Lleyton Hewitt, 110 in the world. I got a chance to play Lleyton Hewitt before he had broken in at a small event. I have to tell you, at that time, having won the match, coming off the court, if you had asked me then, not sitting in this chair (in his office as head pro at Court Sense at Tenafly Racquet Club in New Jersey), I would probably say no. So it was a little surprising for me. To later go on and see him win multiple Slams - because my experience with him was that he hadn't developed his game. He was more of a counter puncher and he didn't have a huge weapon."

"At that time guys were coming on the scene like Goran Ivanisevic, Mark Philippoussis, that had huge weapons. I don't know the timeline of when Hewitt and Philippoussis were coming up but it was somewhat close. So thinking back, actually I probably didn't realize I had taken out a future Grand Slam champion, that I would look back and quote that name over and over again, where people would ask me, How was your career? From a guy, as a journeyman (Note: Geoff Grant produced and created the acclaimed film documentary 'The Journeyman.') And I can always say, Of course, I beat Lleyton Hewitt. They don't have to know that I beat him when he was seventeen [smiles]. It's still a respectable win. And he had won an ATP tournament at that time. I have to agree that it was definitely surprising later, to see him rise to the very top. He was number one, no?"

Question: For two years he was number one. Do you think Hewitt was the best player you ever played?

Geoff Grant: "The best player I ever played...would have to have been Jim Courier. He beat me the worst. And his game was just bigger than mine. It was a terrible match up, again, for me. Similar to the way I was a bad match up for Hewitt. Because he was able to just dictate play and he had a bigger serve than I did. He had everything a little bit better. And then the intimidation factor...his intensity rivaled Hewitt's I think. And that's why he probably stopped playing so quickly, because he burned it even hotter [laughs]. I mean, Courier did."

Question: I watched Courier play a lot on TV. But he didn't seem to express that intensity through the TV like Hewitt did. Maybe through TV you just couldn't see Courier's intensity as clearly?

Geoff Grant: "Yes. On the court the desire to win - I think Courier's up near the top of fierce competitors. Really inside, not necessarily on the outside. Just like Hewitt, you knew you were going to be in a fight. But you knew that Courier pulls zero punches [smiles]. Not that he's not a gentleman but on the court he's just an absolute...ravenous dog [smiles]."

Question: I distinctly remember Jim Courier as a TV commentator using a term like "Step on his throat" which is not a phrase used frequently in the tennis lexicon. I guess it showed a hint of his competitive mindset.

Geoff Grant: "Correct. He'll likely want to kill you on the court. He's a very nice guy. He's a deep guy. He's got a lot of dimensions and I have a lot of respect for him. He's been great for the sport too. Back to Lleyton...Lleyton's in the same breath. But I think the longevity of Lleyton is because he didn't - I don't think it's good or bad, it's different - he didn't have the absolute intensity of a thousand burning suns like Courier, to where the anger would come out. Lleyton's super, super intense on the high level. And it's a different kind of intensity but yet it's still intense."

Question: Any interaction with Hewitt?

Geoff Grant: "Not much. He keeps to himself. And he kept to himself on the Tour. I would think if you know a guy beat you back in the day, you'd still - and then he jumped so far ahead of me - like, okay, I'll be nice to that guy. But he's no longer in my league. So it's not like we're gonna be best buddies. But at the top you don't have a lot of room for a lot of buddies. And he was always a gentleman, always very nice, but there was never any...I never played him again. You'd see him in the locker rooms, he was playing the Tour, I was busy grinding my way up the Challengers and trying to make it on the Tour. So I didn't see him a lot. But when I would see him he was always cordial. I always respected and enjoyed the disposition of the Australians. They're just fun-loving people. They like to enjoy life a little bit more than some of us. And they can see the lighter side of things. Which is a pleasure on the Tour. Hewitt was not necessarily a typical Australian. But he would still crack a smile in the locker room. He wasn't a stoic. Behind closed doors in the locker room he did have a lighter side. But again, because he's such a fierce competitor and it suited him so well, yes, he lives very comfortably in that, like, quiet, reserved world. So that's why you don't ever see much emotion out of him. But I think when he stops you'll see a ton of emotion. Because he most definitely has a soul to him. And he respects what he's doing out there."

Question: Do you have a lasting memory on or off court that captures his essence?

Geoff Grant: "Just the guy that you want to hit that winning shot, the guy you'd like to play doubles with. To be the guy that hangs in there when times get tough. And the guy that's going to snatch the victory if he sees the opportunity. And he's a complete competitor. I think he'll be remembered as a fair competitor. And I think he's living now through his longevity, near the top or at the top still, competing with the top guys...the same thing in a microcosm he does on the court, he'll just hang in there. And I think he just loves what he's doing which continues to allow him to hang in there - and thoroughly enjoy those moments when you don't know where it's going to go with the match. And feel the pain of the match. And go through the emotions of the match. And literally leave it on the court. He embodied that."

Grant leads series 1-0

1998   Winnetka Challenger   Grant 75 63

Chang impressed by Hewitt's "tenacity"

Question: How did you find playing Lleyton? And what was your most memorable match or anecdote involving him?

Michael Chang: "I only played Lleyton twice in my career and unfortunately, it was toward the end of my career. He is a great champion and certainly one of the toughest competitors out there. He has a great game but we all know he's won even more matches because of his tenacity... Lleyton Hewitt has shown himself to be a great champion throughout his career with a fighting spirit that is matched by very few. He should feel great about all he has accomplished."

Hewitt leads series 2-0

2002	'S-Hertogenbosch	R32	Hewitt	76 76
2002	Tokyo	R32	Hewitt	62 62

"He's one of those guys that will always say hello."

Question: Describe your mindset going into your match with Lleyton Hewitt in Newport in 2012.

Tim Smyczek: "I've always looked up to him. He's one of those guys with a similar body type and a similar game. I've watched him play a lot on TV over the years. I knew how good of a player he is on grass. I knew it would be a tough match. I knew I was playing well at the time (ranked no. 180, won first round vs. Denis Istomin 63 63 and three qualifying matches vs. Rishabh Mehra, Ricardo Mello, Danai Udomchoke; just entered top 200 previous month). I wanted to enjoy the match. I knew he was nearing the end of his career so I didn't know if there would be another chance to play him. You know, former number one player in the world, former Wimbledon champion, it was special for me. He's one of the greats of the sport, in my book. I wanted to go out there and play my best."

"I got off to a good start, I played   a great second set. I took him to three sets, had a lot of fun."

Question: What happened in the second set that you were able to have success against him?

Tim Smyczek: "It was a situation where I had a few things fall my way. I got the one break but I felt a lot better. I was able to capitalize on a break point. I made some shots. Unfortunately he seemed to turn it into a higher gear in the third set.   He started returning better. He broke me twice and it was over before I knew it."

Question: Was the match on center court?

Tim Smyczek: "Yes."

Question: Was this the first time you ever played a former world number one?

Tim Smyczek: "I think so, I'm not really sure but probably."

Question: Describe the feeling of walking on the court to play Lleyton Hewitt?

Tim Smyczek: "It was a little daunting. In the player introductions that they do while you're warming up, they went through a very short list of accomplishments for my career and his were obviously a lot longer. It was a bit surreal to hear him announced as a former world number one and former Wimbledon champion, and all the other titles he's won, that was daunting and a little bit embarrassing. The crowd embraced him, as they do pretty much everywhere, he's a fan favorite pretty much worldwide. Before the match even started, it was surreal, a reminder of who I was playing against and how good of a career he's actually had."

Question: Did you have any interactions with Hewitt?

Tim Smyczek: "He told me 'great job' after the match. He was very complimentary in his on-court interview after. Ever since then we've been kind of friends. He's more of a quiet guy, he keeps to himself most of the time. But he's one of those guys that will always say hello."

Question: Please share a lasting memory of Lleyton Hewitt?

Tim Smyczek: "It's kind of funny. But the first two sets of our match he was...I wouldn't say subdued, because I've never seen him on the court when he wasn't really intense. In the third set he broke me in the third game with a return winner - the first break of the third set - and he let out one of his classic 'Come ons.' That was one of those things...I knew it was coming. It sounds funny, as much as I hate to admit it, that was kind of a cool moment [smiles]."

Hewitt leads series 1-0

2012   Newport   R16   Hewitt   64 26 61

The beginning until the end he was completely focused."

Fernando Vicente: "I played him at Queens. He was definitely one of the best players in that moment when I play against him. For me it was like a pleasure because we play on grass courts and he won Wimbledon. I remember it was a good match, he won in three sets. He was amazing from the baseline. No mistakes. Always fighting."

Question: Lasting memory of Hewitt?

Fernando Vicente: "I remember from the beginning until the end he was completely focused, good mentality. That's why I think he was number one. And that's my memory. Not him making shots but very passionate. And it was great to see him."

Hewitt leads series 3-0

2001 Hamburg Masters R32 Hewitt 36 62 64
2003 Scottsdale R32 Hewitt 64 63
2004 Queens R32 Hewitt 46 64 62

"The guy's just fought and fought and fought."

Rick Leach: "The match I remember most about Lleyton was we played in the finals of U.S. Open in 2000. In the third set tiebreaker, Lleyton hit a topspin lob that was so clutch. And it was such a good shot. It basically won the match for them. We ended up losing 7-5 in the tiebreaker. And I saw the fight in this kid. I really realized that he was gonna be something. And he went on to win Wimbledon the next year, number one in the world after that. It showed me a lot. He was a gamer. He showed up. Was able to come up with the big shots when he needed to and he was a fighter. The guy's just fought and fought and fought. I saw it. Because he was so clutch at that point. And I just knew he was going to be a great player after that."

Question: Was Hewitt one of the most intense fighters that you've ever seen in this sport?

Rick Leach: "Yeah. You look at...he's not the biggest guy. He doesn't really have a weapon. He has one of the biggest hearts. I saw that in that match. From there, it was his first

Grand Slam win. I think it gave him some confidence to next go on and win in the singles."

Question: Anything surprise you about him?

Rick Leach: "His longevity. The fact that he's still playing well. Still winning matches. You look at his match today, he won 6-4 in the third (vs. Haase in Key Biscayne). He's been able to endure in a game that's got more and more powerful with bigger and bigger guys. Really, a great player is someone that can be consistent and have good results for a long, long time. And he's done that."

Question: Lasting memory of Hewitt, on or off court? Did you get along well with him?

Rick Leach: "I'm not great mates with him. I have a lot of respect for him. We say hello. I never really spent a great deal of time with him. I just admire his heart and the way he fights on the court. He's probably one of the greatest fighters the sport has ever had."

Question: Pound for pound, Hewitt vs. Nadal, if they're the same size, what happens?

Rick Leach: "Well, that's probably a bad match-up for Lleyton because he'd probably get overpowered by Rafa. I don't know what his record is with him. For what he is, pound for pound, he'd be as good as anybody. Rafa is probably a little too strong for him now. Back in 2001 when Lleyton was number one in the world, it would have been fun to see."

Question: Were there a lot of Come On yells in that US Open final?

Rick Leach: "Yes. Yes [smiles]. He was very fiery. I just

remember the two mini-breaks that we lost in the third set tiebreaker. Max Mirnyi hit a shank return winner that we couldn't read. And then Lleyton hit that topspin lob that was just phenomenal. At the time Ellis (Ferreira) and I had won the Australian Open. I remember beating the Bryans badly in the quarters. So we were playing well. It was a tough match for us to lose because it came down to the one point - the topspin lob by Lleyton was the mini-break that gave them the match. That happens in this game. It was one of the matches that you don't forget. You never will. But at least I was able to win nine other Grand Slams...but it would have been nice to add another one."

"He plays his heart out no matter what."

Igor Kunitsyn: "I played him twice and both times were in Australia. The first was in Adelaide, the second time was Brisbane. So it was fantastic, night sessions in front of his home crowd. And it was great memories for me. Beat him in Adelaide, lost to him in Brisbane. He's a real fighter and a gentleman on the court. He's definitely an Australian tennis legend. It was just a pleasure playing him."

Question: Standout memory of playing Hewitt, anything surprise you about him?

Igor Kunitsyn: "Obviously, everybody watched a lot of

his matches on TV. There's not much you can hide. He did so much for the sport because he always put a hundred percent in everything he does. He works hard. He plays his heart out no matter what. It's just a pleasure playing against such a person."

Question: What were your tactics that enabled you to beat him?

Igor Kunitsyn: "Well, I just had to stick to my tennis. And I think it was I was playing consistent. I was patient because he's one of the best counterpunchers in the game. He has one of the best passing shots in the game. I had to really wait for my chances but not be too offensive. It worked out once, it didn't work out the second time."

Series tied   1-1

| 2007 | Adelaide | RR | Kunitsyn | 46 76 64 |
| 2013 | Brisbane | R32 | Hewitt | 63 46 62 |

"Kinda like a pitbull, unless you put him down, he's not gonna stop biting you."

Dmitry Tursunov: "I've only played him once. And that was a while back. So it's hard for me to say how it is to play him. I don't remember much. I can tell you general things that everybody in the locker room would say about him, if you come up and ask him how to play him. They'll say he's not gonna give you anything, he's gonna fight until the last point. He's a great fighter. Usually against great fighters you have to bring your best game otherwise he's gonna...kinda like a pitbull, he's just gonna...unless you put him down, he's not gonna stop biting you. I guess that would be my expectation if I go out and play him. You have to bring your best game and you have to be ready for a fight. Otherwise it's gonna be a tough day in the office."

Hewitt leads series 1-0

2004   Long Island   SF   Hewitt 63 10 ret.

"He's playing on the Tour with the same anger and everything."

Cyril Saulnier: "I played him in Tokyo. If I remember well, it was a great match. I lost to him in two or three sets. Big, big fighter. It was a great experience. I was playing pretty good. He was a big fighter when he was young. Good, good memory."

Question: Anything surprise you about him?

Cyril Saulnier: "As I said, big fighter. All the time. Pushing himself to the limits. We can see now after many, many years, he's playing on the Tour with the same anger and everything. It's pretty interesting."

Question: Most memorable match versus Hewitt?

Cyril Saulnier: "I played him two times, the second was in Washington. I was real close to winning. I got some chances but it was a great match. Big fight between us. He was always nice with me. Nice guy. He tried to do his best."

Question: Was Hewitt the most intense player you ever played?

Cyril Saulnier: "We can say that. Never giving up, all the time pushing himself to the limit, as I said. And a very good example."

Question: Ever practice with Hewitt?

Cyril Saulnier: "Once or twice. Always nice. Doing his job."

Question: Lasting memory or image of Hewitt?

Cyril Saulnier: "The memory is when he's fighting on the court, you know, yelling Come on all the time. When we talk about Hewitt that's what we think of."

Question: About how many times in your two close matches did Hewitt yell his signature Come on?

Cyril Saulnier: "Oh. I don't remember that [laughs]. I never counted."

Question: A number of times I'd imagine?

Cyril Saulnier: "Yeah. A number of times. A lot [smiles]."

Hewitt leads series 3-0

2000 Basel R32 Hewitt 62 62

2004   Washington   DC   QF   Hewitt   63 36 76
2004   Tokyo   QF   Hewitt   75 61

"My best memory on Tour is actually against him in 2004 when I lost in Bercy."

Gael Monfils: "For me, I think it was always a pleasure because, for me, I grew up with Lleyton because my best memory on Tour is actually against him in 2004 when I lost in Bercy. So I always have this match on my mind. And since then anytime we played against him I was like very happy to see him play. You know, he's just a legend. I think he's a legend. His way to play is very smart. I think he does so many skills, you know, I have big respect for him."

Series tied 2-2

2004   Paris Masters   R32   Hewitt   63 76
2007   Poertschach   SF   Monfils   64 76
2009   Shanghai Masters   R32   Monfils   46 64 62
2010   Wimbledon   R32   Hewitt   63 76 64

"He's one of the players I respect the most on the Tour."

Richard Gasquet: "It's a big fight to play Hewitt because we all know he's a fighter, as one of the best fighters in the world. So I have big respect for him because he's tough so early in his career and he's been enjoying his career and now he's still tough to play. So as I said, he's one of the players I respect the most on the Tour. And he's a legend of tennis and so, of course, it's always a big battle when you have to play against him - you need to win against this guy."

Question: Your most memorable match with Hewitt?

Richard Gasquet: "I think U.S. Open I lost 6-3 in the fifth. Which was fourth round. It was an incredible match. I remember I had cramps, a lot of crowd energy, it was a night session at U.S. Open. So it was an amazing memory."

Question: How do you get along with Hewitt? Do you like him?

Richard Gasquet: "Yes, of course I like him. He's a good guy, of course, I really like him. He's a good person."

Hewitt leads series 2-0

2006   U.S. Open   R16   Hewitt 64 64 46 36 63
2007   Cincinnati Masters   R32   Hewitt 61   32 ret.

"It's like playing a wall."

Xavier Malisse: "It's like playing a wall when you're

young and six years old. That's what it is. It's tough. That backhand always comes back. He fights till the last point. I think that's why he was number one and is still playing today. It's tough to break him down. He's so consistent. When you're facing him you're gonna have to battle, be prepared to be on court two or three hours."

Question: Most memorable match with Hewitt?

Xavier Malisse: "I played my first final against him in Delray. Well, I played him before that. I played him on clay in Delray Beach in '99. Two days final. We had good matches. I know somewhere I was going to play him in Wimbledon finals but that didn't happen [smiles]   (Malisse lost to Nalbandian at 2002 Wimbledon SF 6-7 4-6 6-1 6-2 2-6 - this was the year Hewitt won Wimbledon).   I have good memories. Always been very nice to me also."

Question: Lasting memory of Hewitt on or off court? Did you practice with him?

Xavier Malisse: "I think I played him two or three times. To me, he always said Hi for me. At the end of the day, we're both still people and it's nice to respect one another. That's what I'll take from it."

Hewitt leads series   5-1

1999   Delray Beach   F   Hewitt 64 67 61
2001   Queens   R32   Hewitt 64 63
2003   Cincinnati Masters   R64   Malisse   36 64 62
2004   Roland Garros   R16   Hewitt   75 62 76
2005   Queens   R32   Hewitt 67 75 75

2008   Queens   R32   Hewitt 63 62

"The guy still has the motivation and desire."

Sebastien Grosjean: "It was always great to play against a champion like Hewitt. Always tough, the guy is, you know, a fighter. So it's great he keeps playing in big events. He had an amazing U.S. Open last year, beat Del Potro in five sets. The guy, with all his records, he still has the motivation and desire, so it's great to have Lleyton on the Tour."

Question: Most memorable match with Hewitt?

Sebastien Grosjean: "It wasn't always a great match because Hewitt was better than me [laughs]. But I remember it was always tough. Because the guy - even if he was 40-love down - he wants to win all the points. He was maybe like Rafa today. It doesn't matter what the score - winning points, points, points. He's an amazing player to watch."

Hewitt leads series 6-3

1999	Delray Beach	SF	Hewitt	63 62
1999	Davis Cup	F	Grosjean	64 63
2000	Sydney	R32	Hewitt	64 64
2000	Toronto Masters	R32	Grosjean	76 63
2001	Sydney	SF	Hewitt	63 46 64
2001	Masters Cup Shanghai	RR	Hewitt	36 62 63
2001	Masters Cup Shanghai	F	Hewitt	63 63 64
2001	Davis Cup	F	Hewitt	63 62 63
2003	Queens	QF	Grosjean	63 64

"It's always something special when you play against this guy."

Gilles Simon: "Well, it's always a real challenge because he's a real fighter on the court. I always enjoy to play against him. I have a very good record but it's always a great match. You know it's gonna be like a real fight from the first to the last point.   You know what to expect. And it's always a nice atmosphere on the court. For me it's always a pleasure to play against him. He's one of those players that was number one in the world. He's won Grand Slams. It's always something special when you play against this guy. So I always look forward to play against him."

Simon leads series   4-0

2007   Marseille   R16   Simon 61 32 ret.
2009   Miami Masters   R64   Simon   61 62
2013   Miami Masters   R64   Simon   63   63
2013   Roland Garros   R128   Simon   36 16 64 61 75

"He was a good guy for tennis."

Jo-Wilfried Tsonga: "It's always good to play against a champion. He's won majors. He's got good personality. He was a good guy for tennis. So it's always nice to be against him."

Question: How did you fare against Hewitt?

Jo-Wilfried Tsonga: "For the moment, I won every time. But, you know, it's always close. So I hope I will not play anymore so I will stay on the same percentage of win [chuckles]."

Tsonga leads series 4-0

2007   Queens   R32   Tsonga 76 76
2008   Adelaide   QF   Tsonga 64 62
2012   Wimbledon R128   Tsonga   63 64 64

2014   Davis Cup   Tsonga   63 62 76

Chapter 3:   ATP Players Discuss Lleyton Hewitt in Press Conference Interviews

Spanish team members Alex Corretja and Albert Costa

talk about Lleyton Hewitt before 2000 Davis Cup final in Barcelona.

Q. Alex, do you think there's a danger maybe for the Spanish team that you've actually pumped Hewitt up by the things you've said about him, that he'll be even more determined than before?

ALEX CORRETJA: No. I think he's going to be pretty pumped. No matter if I said that he's behaving on the court, from my point of view, wasn't right. I think he knew it already. He knows the way he is. He knows that he likes to make provocations to the other players. There is nothing new. Maybe I'm the first one to say that, but everybody knew it on the Tour. I don't have anything against him like personally. As he said, and I really agree with him, it's as we're playing here Spain against Australia, not Hewitt against Corretja. If we have to face each other, of course it's going to be a big war to play against each other because of the motivation of winning Davis Cup and maybe afterwards because of our personal situation. But I don't think now we are not going to be any friends. Before we weren't friends anyway. I mean, we just respect each other, say hello, that's all.

Q. If in the first point or the first two or three points of the match, he starts his usual stuff, how do you think the crowd is going to react?

ALEX CORRETJA: I don't know. I would like to see it. But, of course, I think the people wrote about it these days. Some people already told me if I have a fight with Hewitt. I said, " No, I don't have any fight, I just say my point of view." I believe they will react against him pretty hard. But still we have to beat him on the court. No matter if they said something to him or if they whistle him, he's not going to lose because of that. But it can affect him or his game. We will see. I think he's not going to change his personality because I say that. I mean, he doesn't have to. Is the way he is, and that's all. Tomorrow, if he feels that after one game he has to say "Come on" in front of your face, look into your eyes, he will do it anyway.

Q. Albert, what are your views on the way he acts on court?

ALBERT COSTA: Lleyton?

Q. Yes.

ALBERT COSTA: Well, I think he's, like Alex said, a little bit aggressive with the opponent. But for me, I don't care. I didn't look at him. Sometimes I hear "Come on" so loud. But is no worry for me because I didn't want to be in that game.

(Spain defeated Australia in the 2000 Final in Barcelona 3-1.)

Roger Federer discusses Hewitt after beating him   63 64 at 2002 Miami Masters Series semifinal.

THE MODERATOR: Questions for Roger?

Q. You were pretty happy after the previous victory. You must be ecstatic now, aren't you?

ROGER FEDERER: Oh, yeah. I mean, it's nice to play again so well like I did the previous match against (Andrei) Pavel. So I'm really happy. I played a consistent match again and got it through all the way. So this is why I'm working hard for.

Q. Different level of player, though, so it must be particularly pleasing?

ROGER FEDERER: Exactly. It's something special. I've never beaten a No. 1 player before. I've beaten players who were No. 1, but not exactly the time. Plus, I've broken his winning streak and all this. So it's quite a special moment for me, obviously. First Masters Series final, gives me a chance of winning it. So, I mean, it's very nice (smiling).

Q. What is the right tactic against Hewitt?

ROGER FEDERER: I don't think I should tell too much, because, I don't know. It's never good. I better keep this as a secret (smiling).

Marat Safin after losing to Hewitt at 2002 Miami Masters quarterfinal in a third set tiebreaker.

Q. Marat, it was a fantastic match. I know how you feel, but where do you think was the difference? What made the difference tonight?

MARAT SAFIN: My opinion is definitely that the serve make the difference. Because without serve, you're not gonna beat this guy. I mean, he's No. 1 in the world. He's playing great. He has a very good baseline, he has unbelievable legs. Very good anticipation. Very fast, you know. And of course you need to serve much better against him than I served today. I was quite bad. My serve didn't work at all. I think that made the difference in the third set. Because I had an opportunity when I came back at 4-all, I just had to play, you know, my decent service game. I couldn't make it, because he was playing great and returning was just -- I could play with him from the baseline, I was pushing him. I could make some good points. But I need the serve, of course, to beat this guy.

Q. And the difference between the first and second set?

MARAT SAFIN: Oh, the first set just I think that I played good. I didn't make many mistakes. I served okay, pretty okay in the first set. And then, just my percentage of my serves just went -- it was too low. Second and third set, just first set I don't think I put many first serves in. That's the key of the match. Because from the baseline it was perfect. That's why the score was 7-6 in the third. Just I lost by two points, two, three points. So, if I would have serve, you know, in decent way, I think I would have -- I could had the chance to win two sets even.

Q. There was a sensation that after this acrobatics you made and you won the point and you broke, you would have changed the tone of the match?

MARAT SAFIN: Yeah, but it's just I think -- it was like in the movie, you know? Everybody, of course, wish after this jump that you turn the match completely different way and you can -- you have to win this match. But is not, is real life and you have the No. 1 in the world. He's still fighting. He's just still there. Nothing changes. I make the good shot, and that's it. But is not Rocky and is not Rambo.

Q. In the tiebreak, you made some errors off the backhand. Does he just force you to go for those tough shots all the time to the lines?

MARAT SAFIN: Yeah. I think it's also my game. I can't just keep just playing for him from the baseline. I cannot play his game to beat him. I have to do something else, and my game is hitting the ball. That's what I try to do, and that's why I think I was successful still without serve. I was successful. I had some great game to him. That's why it's 7-6 in the third, because I played my game. He tried to play his game. And eventually he won by three points. It's really sad, but it's like this. That's life. He was too good today.

Q. Seems like you had a nice moment at the net with him graciously afterwards. What did you say to him?

MARAT SAFIN: No, just -- just I think it was great match. I said, "Thank you," and just, "Good luck for the tournament." He was too good for me today. That's what I said.

Q. What did he say?

MARAT SAFIN: I don't think he could speak, he would speak but he was excited. And I think it's very happy moment, and it's really nice moment for him. I think was a great match. He played good. I don't think he has to say something. It was just... Was too good. Was a good match today. I think spectators, they would enjoy it very much.

Q. I think it was the best match of the tournament.

MARAT SAFIN: Thank you.

Q. What is it about Hewitt that makes him tough to beat?

MARAT SAFIN: Tough to beat, that he's really consistent, you know - he doesn't lose his mind and he's just playing his game. It's not really impressive game, but he's running, he doesn't make any mistakes, he has really fast hands, fast legs. You cannot play his game. And when he's starting to play his game, it's just baseline, he just kills you. You know, he plays the balls in the right way, in the right place, and it's difficult to play with him, against him from the baseline. He's really, really consistent.

Q. Is there a better fighter on tour than him?

MARAT SAFIN: I don't think so. That's why he's No. 1 in the world.

Q. The one first serve that you did make in the tiebreak was 132 miles-per-hour into his body. How surprised were you that that ball came back?

MARAT SAFIN: I mean, you know that he's probably one of the best -- he has one of the best returns on Tour. You have to serve well against him, you know, to just... just to make free points. So I have to make it -- serve into the body or keep away from him. So it's -- for me, it was, in the tiebreak, was easy to serve to the body than to serve wide because I just -- I lost my serve. I lost the motion.

Pete Sampras after losing the 2001 U.S. Open final to Hewitt 76 61 61.

Q. Were you concerned about something like this happening because of the one-day scheduling?

PETE SAMPRAS: One day, having an off day?

Q. Not having an off day.

PETE SAMPRAS: No, I felt fine. Physically, I was fresh and ready to go. I just ran into another hot player, just like last year. I mean, I tried everything to try to figure it out, and nothing seemed to work. He returned and passed as well as anyone I think I've ever played. But I felt fine.

Q. First set, you both seemed to be struggling to find rhythm and timing. How bad was the wind?

PETE SAMPRAS: It was bad. I mean, I was struggling quite a bit, especially with my serve. It was really blowing pretty good there. You know, it was a struggle. It was a struggle to kind of keep the ball in. But I was really struggling with my serve, because it was that windy. Really it was kind of hard to really get a rhythm out there. You know, he handled it a lot better than I did.

Q. Is this one any more disappointing than last year?

PETE SAMPRAS: This is probably more so because I worked so hard to get here, got through some tough matches and played some great tennis. You know, last year I just got overpowered in a way. Today I just got outplayed. It's disappointing because, like I said, I worked hard to get to the final. It's just tough to kind of put into words right now how I feel, just getting off the court. I'm sure as time goes by, I'll reflect and feel good about what I did here. But only one name gets on that trophy, and it's not mine. So that's the harsh reality of it.

Q. You've given him a lot of credit, but do you feel you were nearly as sharp?

PETE SAMPRAS: Well, the reason I wasn't quite that sharp is because of the way he was returning, the way he was passing. You know, every time I made a second serve, he made me play. I was hitting low volleys. It's hard to do that three sets, let alone I just -- the harder I served, the more I put into it, the better he returned. He's got the best return in the game, the best wheels in the game. He possesses now a much better serve. He's a great player. You'll see him contending here for the next ten years.

Q. You can't sort of shake this off as you had a bad day; he kind of did that to you. Is that more of a concern to you?

PETE SAMPRAS: Yeah, well, last year I really couldn't do anything. This year, pretty much the same story. The reason I wasn't as sharp was because of the way he was playing. He made me work very hard on my service games. He was serving very well. He didn't miss. I mean, I don't know how many errors he hit, but it didn't seem like he missed very often. I thought I hit some good volleys today. He just was there in plenty of time picking off winners left and right. I just wish I could have given a better show for the people. It's disappointing.

Q. Early in the tournament you said a win would salvage your year. Obviously today is a disappointment. The road to get here was very difficult. Do you think to some degree you fulfilled what you wanted? Can you come away with some sense of satisfaction?

PETE SAMPRAS: Well, at this point I have mixed emotions. You're right, I mean, I got through some tough matches, beat some great players along the way. But to get to this point and not get the grand prize at the end is a little deflating. If that had any bearing on today's match, I don't really think so. He was just too good. I mean, I have to give him a lot of credit. He outplayed me. I can still walk out of here with my head up high that I got through some tough matches. But, again, it's also disappointing not to get ultimately, you know, what you want, and that's the title.

Q. How bad was it to lose the first game of the match?

PETE SAMPRAS: It wasn't a great start, especially 30-Love, second serve, hit a serve on the line. The umpire saw it on the line. He didn't overrule it because he couldn't. Too late. That wasn't a start I was looking for. You know, you wanted to set the tone, put some pressure on him. Just got a bad break there. You know, I was serving against the wind, which makes it tough to hold there. I broke him right back, but it wasn't the way I wanted to start off the match, getting down a break early.

Q. You were unable to impose your will on him today with your service game. You had to fall back in some long rallies with him. You weren't able to impose your will with your forehand groundstroke today either. If that had been on today, as it was against Marat and Andre, could we have had a different kind of match?

PETE SAMPRAS: We could have. Could have been a bit closer. But it's tough. You don't want to get in long, grueling rallies with Hewitt. That's his strength. You know, I don't want to get in many of those. I wanted to be aggressive. The times I was aggressive, he came up with some great shots. But I felt fine. I felt fresh. I felt like I could go all night, if I had to. But he loves playing a target. He loves playing guys that come in a lot. He certainly had that today. He uses that quickness to his advantage, passed well, returned well. You know, I was trying to chip and charge a little bit. Wasn't really that effective. Seemed like everything I tried didn't seem to work.

Q. Given the guys that you beat to get to this point, did you feel coming in today that destiny was sitting on your shoulder a little bit?

PETE SAMPRAS: I was hoping a little bit of destiny might have come through for me here. But you have to go out there and compete and win the match. It was a tough road, but a good road, and a disappointing finish.

Q. Have you played anyone who covers the court as fast as Lleyton Hewitt?

PETE SAMPRAS: You know, I put he and Chang in the same league. Those are the two quickest guys I've played. But Lleyton I think possesses, you know, a bit better game.

Q. The first set was difficult. When did you feel that there was a moment in the match where you were getting into dangerous territory?

PETE SAMPRAS: When I lost my serve at 2-1. I had some game points. He broke me at 3-1. That just kind of -- the momentum just kind of went his way, then he broke me again. That was a big turning point. If I could have held on there, maybe make it a little bit closer in the second, maybe he would have played differently, maybe he would have missed a few. That was a bit of a turning point at that 2-1 game.

Q. Is he a better returner than Andre at this point?

PETE SAMPRAS: Yeah.

Q. Why?

PETE SAMPRAS: Because he's quicker. Maybe doesn't have quite the power, but he doesn't miss. You know, he's very tough to ace. He's got the hands and the feet, it's phenomenal. Really pretty impressive stuff.

Q. How do you learn to beat Hewitt? You learned how

to beat Marat after the US Open last year.

PETE SAMPRAS: Well, like Marat, I came in this year a little bit fresher, and he wasn't quite as on. Lleyton, I don't know what I would do differently. I would certainly try to figure that out. Maybe mix up my serves a little bit more, maybe not give him the same pace, same speeds. But when you're in a competition, you do what's comfortable. I always feel like my power's going to come through. The more power I had, the better he returned. It's something you could try, but maybe not as windy a day, I could serve a touch better. It's really hard to say what I would have done differently.

Q. Did he force you to play even more risky with your volleys because he was running down every ball?

PETE SAMPRAS: Yeah, he forces you into a lot of errors. I mean, that's how he wins a lot of his matches. Because he is so quick, you feel like you have to, you know, hit a great volley or hit something on the line. It throws you into a lot of errors from the back court and at net.

Q. Can you talk about the tiebreaker.

PETE SAMPRAS: Yeah, it was good I got back at 3-All. Overrule at 3-All, which was bad timing. Ball was out, but it's still a pretty gutsy call to overrule it at 3-All in the breaker. Hit a great pass at 4-3. Missed a forehand on the top of the tape, missed a pretty easy volley. Just struggling with the wind there at that point. The ball was kind of going on that one side. It was a big point of the match.

Q. Roger Federer, 19 years old at Wimbledon. Lleyton, 20 years old. Andy Roddick is 19 years old. So many other young players out there with so much talent. Does it leave you thinking how difficult it's going to be to win

another Slam with all these young players?

PETE SAMPRAS: It's always difficult winning Slams. I've been fortunate to have won as many as I have. I think I've proven this week that I can still win Slams. There's no question in my mind. There's always going to be younger, you know, stronger, quicker players in all sports. As you get older, it gets more difficult. But, you know, my game is still there. Unfortunately, I just ran into two players, one in Safin last year, and Hewitt this year, that played about as well as, you know, they played throughout the whole tournament. They just saved it for me.

Q. Your backhand volley seemed to be your bread and butter throughout the tournament. Today particularly difficult. You mentioned the wind. Was that primarily the problem on the backhand volley?

PETE SAMPRAS: Yeah, the wind didn't help. But I just -- he forces you into some errors. You feel like if you don't hit it quite firm enough or deep enough, he's going to have an easy pass. Bit of both: a bit of the wind and a bit of his speed.

Q. How impressed are you by Lleyton's focus? A lot of distractions, big match with Roddick.

PETE SAMPRAS: He's a very strong, mentally tough guy. He really had to deal with some off-court stuff, which doesn't help when you're trying to win a Slam. That seemed to settle down. He just got back to business. He's a fighter. That's how he wins his matches. He competes well. He is a great player. He just put everything aside and focused on what he had to do out there. But he should be, you know, feeling pretty good about the way he's competed and the way he played today.

Q. When you look across, you know you're in trouble, late in the match, you see Lleyton there, the way he's playing out of his mind, same with Safin, do you ever think back to '90 and think, "I was there once"? Anything like that go through your head?

PETE SAMPRAS: No, not really. I mean, at that point I'm just trying to hang on, trying to do whatever I can to get back in the match. But it's a great feeling. I felt it a few times over the years. When you're a young guy in your first Slam final, you know, you can just kind of go and play. Sometimes you play great. And he played great today. But I never really reflected during the match.

Q. What is the feeling like when you hit a solid serve, he returns you a solid volley into the corner, and you look up and he's there camped out ready to hit a passing shot down the line?

PETE SAMPRAS: What do you do? If he hits a winner, it's too good. You know, you played a solid point, you couldn't do anything more. You've just kind of got to tip your hat and say, "That's too good." It seemed to happen a lot today. Not much you can do. For strategy, I don't know what I -- I mean, I didn't want to stay back, I had to come in. I just went right into what he loves to do. He loves a target.

Q. You're so good at masking your emotions. But was there a point in this match, maybe last year against Safin, that you said to yourself, "I've tried everything, this just isn't my day, he's so confident that it doesn't matter what happens"?

PETE SAMPRAS: It was a similar feeling to last year because, you know, last year I was a bit overpowered. Like

I said, this year I was outplayed. When I lost my second serve -- when I got down two breaks in the second, I just felt it slipping away. I just felt, "Wow, he's playing great." I was just kind of struggling to hold on to serve. He was making me work. I didn't have the answers. When the third set came around, he just kind of maintained it. I was really hoping to kind of try to hang on there, maybe he might get tight, maybe he might miss a few, maybe I could get my game going, get the crowd involved. Didn't happen. He just maintained that focus and play, just like Safin did.

Q. Australia has such a tremendous tennis tradition. Can you see him in that tradition? Are there ways that he's an Aussie out there on court?

PETE SAMPRAS: Well, as far as his game?

Q. Yes.

PETE SAMPRAS: Well, most Aussies are serve and volleyers. Lleyton is more of a counter-puncher, baseliner. There's not a lot of similarities between, say, Hewitt and Rafter. But what he does is very effective. He plays with a lot of heart, a lot of tenacity. But I wouldn't consider him like kind of a typical Australian player. He's more of a counter-puncher.

Q. He won the coin toss, elected to let you serve. Were you surprised by that or was the wind that big of a factor?

PETE SAMPRAS: No, I wasn't surprised. All the great returners - Andre, Lleyton - they like to return first, which I love. I like serving, setting the tone early. Just got off to a bad start. Even though I broke him back, I didn't like the fact that I lost that game. He kind of set the tone like he was on my serve and passing well when he broke me there.

Q. Do you find this stadium harder to play in than the previous stadium?

PETE SAMPRAS: Yeah.

Q. Is it because of the wind?

PETE SAMPRAS: Yeah.

Q. Yesterday Marat said he was so impressed by your performance, he said the final is all up to you. Was that wrong?

PETE SAMPRAS: Well, it is up to me because Lleyton, he lets you play a little bit. But if you're not playing well or not quite on top of your game, he's probably the most difficult guy to play because he doesn't miss. He doesn't give you any free points. As much as it's up to me, he kind of had all the answers for everything that I tried, from picking off my serve to hitting great passing shots. It was kind of just too good. Really give him a lot of credit.

Carlos Moya at Australian Open 2001.

Q. I was just wondering if you find yourself playing Lleyton Hewitt in the next round, what you think of that match?

CARLOS MOYA: Well, it will be interesting and pretty exciting I will say. Because he's a great player. He's playing very well. First round was very tough for him, and you know, I'm very confident. I think if I'm playing the same level I am playing right now, I am able to beat him. Why not? It will be a great match. But he still has a tough opponent which is (Tommy) Haas, you never know what is going to happen. But if Hewitt is the winner, I'm going to be ready for that match.

Q. There's been a lot written about the way he behaves on the court. Do you find it at all distracting because he's so fairly loud, disputes calls and carries on a bit sometimes?

CARLOS MOYA: Well, it's not really, you know, he doesn't make you feel comfortable about that. But I think he's not fake at all. He does it because that helps him to increase his level, to play better, and I don't think he does it to bother his opponent. But he does it because it pumps him up a lot. And, you know, he's happy being like that and I have nothing to say about that because he's doing that for himself, not to bother the opponent.

Moya after defeating Hewitt in third round...

CARLOS MOYA: Well, has been a great match not only today but the last three matches I've been playing very well. And I know after the match I won today is unbelievable. I have no words to describe it. I never gave up. I was two sets to one down and I knew was gonna be complicated to come back. And, you know, as I said, I never gave up. I kept fighting. And at the end, I've got paid off. You know, it's unbelievable, the feeling of being the winner of this match. And, you know, I'm not -- I just won three matches. Still many matches left to win the tournament, and, you know, that's why I came here. And I want to be focus on the next match because I didn't win anything yet, so I have to go step by step and, you know, but I have to say that is gonna give a lot of confidence, the victory, for sure.

Q. Is it not just the victory, but the way you played. Is that almost as important?

CARLOS MOYA: Yeah, I played very well, very aggressive. I knew that if I was playing from the baseline the whole match it was gonna be really tough. I had to go to the net very often. I think I volleyed very well today, I served very well. My forehand work very well, and, you know, maybe my backhand was at the beginning a little bit not working that well. I saw the thing that was indoor at the beginning, I didn't feel the ball the same way as I was feeling on the last days. But, you know, I have to be very proud of the way I've been playing, and great victory for me.

Q. Did your mind at any stage go back to your match with (Todd) Martin in New York last year which must have been a real terrible blow for you to lose in those circumstances?

CARLOS MOYA: The match was tough because it was last 16, US Open, and I had the matchpoint. I was very close to beat him and then he beat me. But you just try to forget the bad memories you have been having lately and just focus on the next match and never came to my mind that I was gonna lose the same way I lost against Martin. And, you know, just kept fighting. I could not show my feelings on court, but everything was going inside my body, and, you know, after I won the last point, it was great. But, no, I wouldn't say that those memories came to my mind.

Q. How hard is he an opponent? How difficult is he an opponent?

CARLOS MOYA: He's very difficult. He runs like crazy,

and all the balls are coming back and, you know, I've been lucky that I got many free points with my serve. And my feeling was very good, but he's a very tough player, and mentally he's the No. 1. And as I said, maybe he doesn't have the talent of Safin or Kuerten, but mentally he's the No. 1 in the world I would say. He never gives up, and he's always there.

Q. You said you didn't show your feelings, but Lleyton certainly did on a few occasions. Did you take that into account?

CARLOS MOYA: No. No, because I don't have any problem with him. I respect him. We're just different. I don't show my feelings and he show his feelings. He gets a lot of support from the crowd because he's playing here and he needs to motivated. I think that's why he's doing that. But he is not doing that just to bother me or he has respect for me, I think, and for the Open. And, you know, was a moment when, I think it was a bad call for him that he kind of complained to the referee. But with me, he didn't have any problem. And, you know, we just had a great match and we are just different. You know, I don't show my feelings.

Juan Martin Del Potro calls Hewitt his tennis hero.

I first did a Biofile interview with Juan Martin Del Potro in 2008 at the U.S. Open. The first question I asked him was: Who were your childhood heroes?

Del Potro answered swiftly and simply, "Lleyton Hewitt."

Since learning that information, I have noticed that whenever the two play, there is always enormous respect given, especially by Del Potro to his hero Hewitt. It almost appears Del Potro sort of defers to Hewitt sometimes.

Their clash at the 2013 U.S. Open on Arthur Ashe Stadium in a second round night match was a fascinating duel. Hewitt eventually triumphed in five sets from a 2-1 deficit. At the climax of the battle, Del Potro embraced and showed tremendous admiration, also speaking a few kind words to his "hero." It looked like big brother/little brother love.

To my eyes, it appeared that a small part of Del Potro was actually happy to lose to Hewitt, his hero...to help give him a positive push at the end of his illustrious career.

It has to be difficult for Del Potro to want to thrash a player he respects so much like his hero Hewitt.

Minutes after this match, at the press conference, I popped the first two questions to Del Potro…

Q: Describe the feeling to play your number one hero Lleyton Hewitt.

Juan Martin Del Potro: It's special, but just before the match, when we go to the court, never think about my opponents. I just try to play my game, to feel good myself. I think tonight was a really tough battle for both, but in the end he play better. He play impressive. The tiebreak on the fourth set he made a very good passing shots. I mean what I say before: he's a great champion and a great fighter. For the second round, it's a really difficult player.

Q: Is a little part of you happy to see him win?

Del Potro: Of course not, but I wish all the best. I like when he's winning and when he's doing well, he's healthy. He play like he has a chance to go far in this tournament. Of course, I wish him all the best. I have a good relationship. He's a very good player to play, and that's it.

Juan Martin Del Potro's Wimbledon 2009 press conference after playing Hewitt for the very first time, losing 36 57 57.

Q. Did Lleyton surprise you with the level of his play?

JUAN MARTIN DEL POTRO: Yes, he play very good. We play a high-level match. I play good, too, but was not enough to beat him.

Q. What gave you a problem about his game? What were the problems he caused you?

JUAN MARTIN DEL POTRO: Well, is difficult for me playing this kind of surface. And Lleyton has much more experience than me. He has many matches here in grass court. He was a champion here. So I need time to learn how can I play on this surface, and that's it.

Q. You were very warm in your congratulations to him at the net. Can I ask what you said?

JUAN MARTIN DEL POTRO: Well, I say, Congrats. He did a very good match. You know, he's one of my idols. And I say, You are in very good shape again, so I'm happy for you and good luck.

Q. Did you think before this match that you had an opportunity against a player who is finding his form

again? This was an opportunity for you, wasn't it?

JUAN MARTIN DEL POTRO: Yes, I think so. I have good things to get about this match. I learned little bit playing with him.
You know, he never miss a returns when he has a break, and I did many times. So I think that was the difference between me and him.

Q. When you say Hewitt is one of your idols, how long have you been aware of him or followed his career?

JUAN MARTIN DEL POTRO: I start to follow him was when I was young, like 11 years, 12 years.

Milos Raonic's 2012 Australian Open press conference after losing to Hewitt 64 36 67 36.

"I started out nervous. I struggled more with him than I did with anything else really. He was keeping the ball very low. He was hitting always constant pace and quite low. Even when he was defending, he was always defending low. At the beginning I was trying a little too much just to go through rather than getting down and playing a little bit more conservatively and getting down and sort of hitting the ball the right way. I don't want to get into it technically, but...and then after that you could see his belief start to grow more and more. He's a very smart player. He knows how to win. When he smells a little bit of weakness he just really pounces on it and knows how to expose it. He's not the type of player that will give you really anything. Doesn't matter how hurt he's been, how old he is, he's as much a competitor as he ever was. He got me with that."

Chapter 4: Lleyton Hewitt Press Conference Interviews

Lleyton Hewitt's interview after defeating Todd Martin in July 1999 in Boston in his first Davis Cup singles match 64 67 63 60.

Q. Second set tiebreak. The way it went, how do you get yourself back in the match, third set?

LLEYTON HEWITT: I thought Todd was starting to get a little bit tired at that point and really I think that was the most positive thing I could take out of it; that whatever I am feeling, I am sure he is feeling a lot worse than I am. So I went out there with that attitude for the rest of the match. I was going to stay out there as long as I had to to win that first match.

Q. How does match rate in terms of your performance?

LLEYTON HEWITT: Best win I have ever had.

Q. How was your night last night?

LLEYTON HEWITT: Actually pretty tough to go to sleep last night. Trying to have an early night, but then really couldn't get to sleep for a couple of hours. I just got on the phone; called the folks back home and all the mates.

Q. Todd was struggling the fourth set. Did you sense that as well; that pretty much he was spent?

LLEYTON HEWITT: Yeah, Newc (Captain John Newcombe) sort of felt that as well. I had to really try and get on top of him early in the fourth set. I did that; I came up with a few good returns and he hadn't been serve and volleying any second serves up 'til then until the first game of the fourth set; then he started serve and volleying second serves, so I took out of that that he really wanted the points to finish quickly and didn't want to sort of get into a baseline rally with me.

Q. Is it what you had expected it to be?

LLEYTON HEWITT: Pretty much. I can't wait to get out there and play again. Fantastic atmosphere out there. I tried to block the crowd out as much as I could today. All that band noise, stuff really sort of got over the top of our Fanatics up the top there, didn't really hear them at all.

Q. How did you manage to keep your nerve throughout the match?

LLEYTON HEWITT: I think Newc had a big part in that, sort of he kept me pretty calm, taking deep breaths at every change of ends and no matter what the situation was, straight off, after I lost the second set when I got the early break in the first set, when I was still serving for 5-Love in the fourth, Newc was great on the side of the court.

Q. Your experience at Wimbledon playing on Center Court with Becker, even though it was a loss, did that help you in any way just going through that?

LLEYTON HEWITT: I think it helped me, but I think the biggest thing was the match I played against Todd in Sydney. I took a lot of confidence out of that match. I was pretty tired at that time and just made the final of Adelaide; that was the quarterfinals of Sydney; then I came out and I really gutsed that out. I think that was in the back of Todd's mind that I wasn't going to go away out there today. So I think really that match actually did a lot for me even though I did lose it.

Q. How high are you right now on your Davis Cup debut and can you also talk about the atmosphere out there?

LLEYTON HEWITT: It is fantastic. As I said, it is the biggest win of my career. Biggest match I have played in my career. I am sure there is a lot of people back home watching it into the wee hours of the early morning. It is a great atmosphere out there on center court, out here in Boston as well. It is just -- because it is pretty tight as well. You sort of got your guys up on one end; I sort prefer being on the far end as much as I can. Come down the other end and it is: "Todd, Todd, Todd," so, I try to block out the crowd as much as possible, but you still hear it.

Q. Do you pattern your game after Agassi at all?

LLEYTON HEWITT: A little bit. I try to play pretty aggressive from the baseline. I think the biggest thing today was my serve. I served really well. But I don't think I actually just model my game on one person. I try and work on a lot of areas of my game. I am trying to become and all-court player.

***

Todd Martin's comments about Hewitt after the match.

Q. He doesn't seem flustered by big occasions, whatever, is that just how these young guys are these days?

TODD MARTIN: No, I don't think you can generalize young guys. I don't think you can generalize anyone. I think Lleyton is one of the few people in the tennis world that have very, very, very great nerves. He sees big occasions and he attacks them and I don't think -- I don't think he reacts at all negatively to any situation. He is a positive thinker and he is confident. It is like Pete, one of the reasons Pete is such a great player is he has got fabulous nerve.

Q. Is that because he is 18 years old, Todd?

TODD MARTIN: No, I told you it is not because of the youth. It is simply because it is a nature thing. You got 17 year olds that could choke their tail off and you got 40 year olds that are great competitors.

Q. What do you see as his future; do you see him getting to the top?

TODD MARTIN: Well, he -- I am not clairvoyant, but he is certainly is better today than he was in January when I played him. I assume that that progress will continue to be made and, you know, maybe he just matched up well with me today, I don't know. It is hard to say whether he is going be one of the top five players in the world. He is always going to have the ability to beat great players. But to end up doing what Pete, Andre, Jim, Patrick, these guys do, it is week in and week out, and that remains to be seen. But I couldn't have been more impressed with his performance today.

Lleyton Hewitt interview after losing first match at 1999 Davis Cup final to Cedric Pioline in Paris 76 76 75.

Q. What made the difference out there?

LLEYTON HEWITT: You know, I think it comes back to serving at 5-4 in the first set. You know, I had him on the ropes then. That's when I really had to sort of dig deep and get the first couple points on my serve, put him under pressure. It was much like the Paris Indoors where I served for the set, goes into a tiebreaker. Tiebreaker, he's all over me. Eventually I have a chance. Also I was up a break early in the first set which I was 40-Love up on my service game, let it slip there. That was a crucial game because I felt like I was on top of him then. I felt like I was going to be the fitter guy out there today. You know, if I could get one, two sets - for him to win in four or five sets, I think, was going to make it tough for him; particularly the way the sets were going, how long they were going.

Q. Give us your resume of the first day's play, John?

CAPTAIN NEWCOMBE: Well, it's finished up as perfect from the Davis Cup, I guess, general standpoint of it's one match all, poised tomorrow for what should be an unbelievably exciting doubles match. Philippoussis walks away, you know, feeling pretty good about the way he's played, as Pioline walks away feeling pretty good. But I think from Lleyton's point of view, he knows he could play a little better than he did in the first set and a half, and, you know, he could have been up the first set if he had won the first set, then he had the chances, two breaks early, a set point, served a double-fault. If he'd won the first set, things could have been different. I don't think when he reflects tomorrow he'll say, "I could have done a little better, but the other guy played as great as he could play." I think

Lleyton will be confident going into Day 3 if he has to play the decider. I know from my point of view, I feel pretty good about what he did out there today.

Q. How do you feel about how you did out there today, Lleyton?

LLEYTON HEWITT: I felt like I was fighting the whole day. You know, I couldn't seem to just get that breakthrough, that one piece of luck or whatever it may be that, you know, really sort of opened up the match for me, whether it was on breakpoints - it happened every set - the double-fault I suppose in the first set tiebreaker, then I sort of worked my way back into the second set tiebreak as well. In the third set, I get back to 5-All and had, gee, it felt like 50 breakpoints on it, I couldn't break him. The whole match, even when I was 5-1 down in the third set, I felt if I could get one set, I was going to win the match. I just couldn't get that breakthrough, as I said. It just felt so hard for me today to, you know, come up with the right shots on the big points.

Q. I guess you said it was easy for you to play with the crowd against you. How tough or easy was it to play against Cedric today?

LLEYTON HEWITT: What was that?

Q. You've been quoted to say that you would prefer to play with the crowd against you.

LLEYTON HEWITT: No.

CAPTAIN NEWCOMBE: It's a misquote.

LLEYTON HEWITT: Misquote, I think. I'd love to play the crowd with me anytime.

Q. How tough was it to play against Cedric today?

LLEYTON HEWITT: He played great. You know, he mixed it up very well today; came up with big serves on big points when he needed to. You know, you got to take your hat off to him. You know, I think it comes back to he's played in the Davis Cup final before. You know, he knows what it's all about. You know, I suppose you can't buy experience.

Q. Story of today really was that you were on the brink so many times of "getting" Cedric - so close to breaking him; got to two tiebreaks and he won them both. How psychologically draining is that?

LLEYTON HEWITT: It was very tough out there at the time. As I said, I felt like even when I was two sets to love down, if I could just sneak out the third set, I felt like I was going to win the match. At no time during the match did I feel like it was over. You know, I kept telling myself, you know, "We're in this match." You know, I thought I was playing at times a lot better than he was, yet I was a bit unlucky. He would hit some great angle volleys on big points. You know, just little things. He shanked a couple balls over my head which I couldn't get to. You know, just felt like a lot was going against me at the time.

Q. Is there anything you take out of that that you think will help you on Sunday if it comes down to you?

LLEYTON HEWITT: It's the worst feeling I've ever had as a tennis player, losing a Davis Cup match. I can say I don't want to have this feeling again. You know, I can take so many things away from today's match, whether it be how to handle the crowd. Everyone can talk about how loud the crowd is going to be. Until you're actually out there playing in the middle of it, you got no idea. For me to experience that today, you know, if it does come -- I hope it doesn't come down to my match for the team's point of view, but if it did come down on my match on Sunday, I can say I'd handle everything a lot better.

***

Cedric Pioline's comments about Hewitt after the match:

Q. What do you think about Hewitt? He seems unique on the circuit.

CEDRIC PIOLINE: He plays well. There's no mystery. He's very fast. He's a very good fighter. I believe his game is very tiring also, so I'm not sure he will be able to play every year, year after year, in the same way. All the players will start to know him a little bit better; know his weaknesses and his strengths. But it's true that when he plays that way, he's very good.

***

Guy Forget's comments about Hewitt after the match:

Q. How is Cedric now? What did he feel on the court when Hewitt was coming back?

CAPTAIN FORGET: Well, he was frustrated because Hewitt was coming back. He was seeing that Hewitt had a bit of luck. He was thinking, "I can't believe it." He was starting to be worried. But I gave him the truth. I said, "Just believe in the quality of your game. You're playing at a very high level, and he is incredible. He's playing perfectly. You have nothing to be concerned with. You don't have to be angry at yourself because you're doing your best. You're doing the maximum you can do. This is the law of the sport." I hope it helped him because after that particular moment, he reacted and he continued and continued trying; he didn't give up. In the moment, he could fall into a hole, because of the frustration. When you are up 5-1 and you have a match point, and then the other one comes back, it's very difficult. They played three hours and 40 minutes for three sets. Also they were a bit tired. There was a lot of tension.

Q. Hewitt said if he had won the third set, he would have won the match.

CAPTAIN FORGET: No, I'm not sure of that. I think Cedric was ready to play one or two sets more. The other one played the end of the third set in a phenomenal way. I don't believe Hewitt would have been able to maintain that level until the end of the match. He would have had ups-and-downs. When you are two points away from a match, when you are at three sets, winning a match, it's a great difference. I think it's incredible saying that.

    ***

Lleyton Hewitt interview after defeating Albert Costa 36 61 26 64 64 in the first singles match of the 2000 Davis Cup final in Barcelona.

LLEYTON HEWITT: Haven't had a lot of time to reflect on it so far. It's the best feeling I've ever had. You know, it is a dream come true again. It feels like I say this all the time. This is the biggest thing in my tennis career so far by a mile. You know, I remember warming up with Stolty a couple years ago for the Davis Cup, I was the orange boy, about 15 years old. He said, "You'll have your best moments in Davis Cup tennis and you'll have your worst moments in Davis Cup tennis throughout your whole tennis career." There's no doubt that so far to date, the one lost that I lost in a live rubber last year to Pioline was the worst feeling I've had on a tennis court. Then this year, you know, it's amazing how one year and it's all changed.

Q. Were there some tears at the end? You're walking back to serve for the match. They're jeering you as you walk back. Love-40 down, jeering every move you make. How do you get your mind around that and focus?

LLEYTON HEWITT: It was the toughest thing I've ever had to do in tennis, I think. I looked over at Newc and the boys on the sideline. They're pumping you up, but they're like a little bit disappointed because two minutes ago you were serving for the match in the fifth set. This feeling came through. You know, "You can still get this." That's the most positive I've ever stayed in a game like that. I was telling myself just to block out the crowd, not let it affect me. I knew Costa wasn't going to do anything with the next three points that he had breakpoint opportunities. He was tight as ever out there. I knew if I went out there and I served a couple of good first serves, if I stayed aggressive and made him come up with the passing shots, I could still get out of that game. That's what ended up happening.

Q. How about your own stamina? It was pretty tight. Strong test of your fitness.

LLEYTON HEWITT: It was unbelievable. In the interview

I did with Fitzy after the match, I just said there was a question mark over how long I was going to last out there. I've done very little practice since Toronto, since I started feeling ordinary. I just went out there, played a match, warmed up 15 to 20 minutes before the matches. I wasn't able to do the yards. I've done as much as I've ever done, more than over the last 22 weeks. I definitely wasn't giving myself the greatest preparation due to this illness. You know, it's an unbelievable feeling that I was down and I was hurting, I got my second wind, I was able to guts it out and come through with the goods.

Q. You said at the end the crowd were the most difficult you've had to face. At the beginning, you went 5-Love down pretty quickly. They were on your back as soon as you walked onto the court. Did that have any bearing on you going down 5-Love?

LLEYTON HEWITT: No, that had no bearing. You know, obviously it was pretty tight out there. I think we were both pretty tight. I looked at it, you know, I kept telling Newc, "I have breakpoints, game points." Really the first set I felt I should have won 6-3, the total opposite. Out of the first four or five games, I had game points in three of them. I felt like I wasn't playing my best tennis. You know, I think the second set I really stepped it up right from the start, ended up winning six out of seven games when I came back from 5-Love down. I felt like, you know, I let him off a little bit of a hook at the start of the third set. I had a lot of deuce chances the first two or three of his service games.

Q. Do you think the crowd went too far at any time?

LLEYTON HEWITT: Definitely that last game was the worst I've ever seen. You know, if they're going to have a rule that you give out point penalties or whatever for the crowd going over the top, you know, I don't think it will come any worse than that. I think, you know, someone's got to step up and say something. We've been talking in the locker room. You know, the worst crowd -- not the worst crowd, but the worst game or noise between points, I literally had to serve, play the first point, the first shot, even the second shot I had to play, you know, was still played in a lot of noise out there. You know, I definitely feel it's probably a little bit out of order.

Q. Do you feel in Davis Cup games that the crowd etiquette could be different, rules go out the windows compared to other tournaments?

LLEYTON HEWITT: I think a little bit. All the past matches, I think France was loud last year, but they didn't go over the line I don't think at all. This is the first time I think that, you know, we -- I don't mind a bit of whistling between first and second serves. Some tournaments you've got to put up with that if you're playing the home guy anyway. We're used to putting up with that. When you're actually playing the whole rally, it's not a soccer match out there.

Q. Do you think the Australians feel that Corretja not playing, that decision by Spain, has played into your hands a little bit? Does that suit you all?

LLEYTON HEWITT: You know, it's hard to say. I think we definitely thought that Alex was going to play on the first day. There's no doubt about that. He's got the best ranking, he's the most experienced out of everyone. If you look at the match-ups, you can understand why they put Costa against me. It's the only clay court match that I've played against any of the Spaniards, and he won that at Roland Garros. Ferrero, you know, he's not the typical

Spaniard. He does hit very heavy off the baseline, but he's a very good counter-puncher and good returner, as well. You can understand their thinking a little bit, sort of to put him against Rafter, as well. But it is a big call in Davis Cup not to have your No. 1 player on rankings in the team.

Q. Did you say anything to Pat or did Pat say anything to you before he went out and you came back in?

LLEYTON HEWITT: Boys get pretty crazy when you go back in the locker rooms after you've had a win. You know, Pat just said, "Gutsy win, mate." I just said, "Good luck. Let's try to finish this day one on a good note." It's hard I think for a person in Pat's situation out there. You know, after the team has had such a good win, he's been waiting in the locker room for four and a half hours before he gets to go out there. This morning with the opening ceremonies, he's all ready to go, he's got to sit back, wait, have a lot of nerves. It's a tough situation. You've got to block that out and try to go out there and do the job, as well.

Q. When you won the last point, were you feeling you had a little bit of the Davis Cup already in your pocket?

LLEYTON HEWITT: That's a big call. We're only into the first match of the tie. Definitely it was a great start, though, for the team. Just to get the momentum and really show the Spanish that we're here to play.

Q. What did Newc say to you? It looked as if he was almost in tears when you came off.

LLEYTON HEWITT: After the match?

Q. Yes.

LLEYTON HEWITT: He was very emotional. Newc,

thought he wouldn't stop hugging me (laughter). Obviously, those guys have been through a lot. He played a major part in the role today in me winning, just with the health situation and everything under the control. Just to have a guy who I'm sure he's been in so many situations the same as that before when you're not feeling a hundred percent, trying to push through it, sitting next to you, it's a huge bonus.

Q. You changed quite a few racquets at quite interesting times. What makes you change it and want to get a new one?

LLEYTON HEWITT: You know, it's just a matter of I'm playing with natural gut. Once it starts cutting through the gut, I put a couple of string-a-lings in there, but I'll never let myself -- I can't say "never." Most times I don't want to let myself break a string on a big point. I'll put a few in there. It actually makes the racquet a little bit deader, as well. Sometimes you actually don't time the ball as well when you have a lot of string savers in the racquet. You know, I just try and -- when I can see it's going to go on the next three, four points, it's time to change.

Q. Were you aware that their captain was getting quite boisterous about it?

LLEYTON HEWITT: Yeah, mate. He had a lot to say about everything, today. It wasn't going to worry me one way or the other.

Q. How much do you owe to Newc and how much does Australia owe to Newc for his captaincy over the last few years?

LLEYTON HEWITT: A hell of a lot. You know, firstly for me, he took me under -- he and Rochey both took me sort of under their wing. My first Davis Cup tie was in Sydney where we beat France. Just hanging out with the guys, practicing a bit, picking up balls, getting their drinks, it's just fantastic to be a part of it all and be wearing an Australian Davis Cup jacket or track suit. You know, I owe so much to those guys. Not only have they helped me through Davis Cup matches, but also my career. They're one of the main reasons, with all the other coaches and family and everyone who has -- that's one of the main reasons why I've reached sort of the Top 10 in my career at such a young age.

Q. How much is that win going to -- what is it going to do for your confidence coming into Sunday? How much is it going to boost your confidence? Secondly, how sure are you that you'll be playing Corretja?

LLEYTON HEWITT: You know, it's obviously a huge boost, not only for me, but for the team, as well. It's one of those matches, so tight, you feel like you're always down, then you get over the last hurdle and actually win is a great feeling for the team. Obviously, I feel like I'm hitting the ball quite well on clay, I'm moving well. It's nice to know I have the stamina, as well. With Corretja, who knows? You know, I think a lot's got to do with the match that's going on with Pat and Ferrero and also the doubles tomorrow, you know, who he chooses to play. Is Costa up to playing a fifth match if it came down to it? We don't know.

Q. Psychological warfare in Davis Cup. How much sweeter is that after the comments that Alex made this week, if at all?

LLEYTON HEWITT: You know, I've had to put up with comments in the past. I haven't faltered at them so far. You know, I don't understand why people open their mouths all the time. I mean, I get pumped up on the court anyway. It's not going to stop me at all. You know, to look over and see that their No. 1 player is sitting on the sidelines on day one not playing, I think that gives everyone a lot of confidence in our team.

Lleyton Hewitt interview after losing to Juan Carlos Ferrero 62 76 46 64 to lose the Davis Cup to Spain in 2000.

Q. How emotional was that for you today?

LLEYTON HEWITT: You know, it's obviously very hard to take, especially being the one out there to actually lose the Davis Cup. You know, two days ago I was saying I had the greatest feeling out on that court, and now it's probably the worst feel in my tennis career so far. How things change so quickly. I felt like I gave 100% out there today. You know, I've been struggling coming into this Davis Cup. You know, I gave everything I had in both matches. I couldn't have asked any more of myself.

Q. Were you pretty tired towards the end?

LLEYTON HEWITT: I felt as good at the end as I did at the start. Obviously, the body was pretty stiff after the five-setter two days ago. You know, I felt if I could have got out of that fourth set, I would have won the fifth. He gave everything that he had. To his credit, he came up with some big points at the right time. Obviously, with such a big crowd behind him, as well, he knew he was only a game or two away at that stage. It's tough to stop someone in that situation.

Q. How were the crowd today? A lot better than it was

on Friday?

LLEYTON HEWITT: No, pretty much the same. I think they kept a pretty poor standard the whole way through. You know, it's definitely a lot worse than Nice last year, that's for sure.

Lleyton Hewitt interview after winning first round in Hamburg 2001 against Arnaud Di Pasquale 63 62.

Q. Lleyton, was there some sense of relief to get through a match like that because it was a bit scrappy, a lot of breaks of serve?

LLEYTON HEWITT: Yeah, I thought it was pretty good tennis though. That is the best he has every played against me. I played him a lot in juniors; played him once in the seniors and won last year in Rome. Forehand is big out there. Such tough conditions out there. The balls are so heavy and the clay is so slow out there and especially today with the moisture in the air, it's one of the slowest places I have ever played tennis in. So yeah, I am just happy to get through.

Q. Is it mainly because of the weather that the conditions are like that or were they like that when you were practicing in the sunshine?

LLEYTON HEWITT: A lot has got to do with the weather. The German clay is a definite slower clay than the French Open clay. That has always been the case, I think, but here in Hamburg you get that moisture hanging over the court as well. It was pretty slow when I went out there to warm up this morning.

Q. When you had the break after the Davis Cup did you do much training and what did you do?

LLEYTON HEWITT: No, not a lot. I put the rackets down and just rested up basically. Last year was such a long year with the Olympics and obviously making it through the Davis Cup final; then starting back in Adelaide I had felt like I hadn't had a break so just put the rackets down for a couple of weeks and went out to the movies, stuff like that. It's good to be back on the Tour right now.

Q. Do you feel that Davis Cup helped you a lot for the clay court season?

LLEYTON HEWITT: No doubt it's helped me to be able to reflect on those matches and instill that confidence on clay that I beat Gustavo Kuerten. I didn't lose a set in three days of tough -- I don't think the pressure gets any tougher when playing Davis Cup tennis; let alone playing in Brazil against the best player in the world. Not dropping a set for those nine sets in a row is a pretty good achievement. I can definitely reflect on that and draw strength from that going into the French Open.

Q. Do you feel rejuvenated by the break that you have had? Do you feel fresher?

LLEYTON HEWITT: Yeah, it is always hard coming off a break the first week and normally I do pretty well, but coming onto clay it's always tough if you haven't put out a lot of hours I think. That is why this preparation - I played Rome, Hamburg, two big tournaments on the calendar; then I go to Dusseldorf which I am guaranteed a lot of matches and good matches against very good clay court players, going into the French so hopefully that is going to hold me in better form going in. Clay is one of those surfaces which it's quite hard to sort of get in a rhythm, sliding and stuff. So last week, even though I did lose, then I got to play a couple of good claycourters and that gives me a little bit more confidence.

Q. So you are reasonably happy at this stage of the clay court season?

LLEYTON HEWITT: Yeah, I feel like I am getting better and better. Today I felt like for the conditions, I hit the ball great. There is still a few areas of my game that I need to work on, but I have still got a couple of weeks before really start settling in in Paris.

Q. Will you be playing with Pat next week in Dusseldorf?

LLEYTON HEWITT: Yeah, we are playing together.

Lleyton Hewitt Interview after beating Jonas Bjorkman in five sets at Australian Open 2001.

Q. How's the body feeling after that epic one?

LLEYTON HEWITT: Yeah, well, you know, it was a very tough match physically and mentally out there tonight. It's just sort of wait and see really how it pulls up tomorrow, and then hopefully on Thursday I'm going to be, you know, 90 to 100 percent again.

Q. The treatment you had, was that for the hamstring?

LLEYTON HEWITT: Yeah. I twinged, sort of twinged it a little bit during practice a couple days ago, basically when I first arrived here in Melbourne. So that was a bit of a concern going into the match as well tonight. I've been getting treatment sort of basically ever since I've been here in Melbourne and it just wasn't getting any better out there on the court tonight, so I needed something out there. You know, it's something that I just had to put, you know, play through out there.

Q. With all that in mind, does it worry you how much you might have left for the other rounds, particularly with your hard second-round opponent to start off?

LLEYTON HEWITT: It's just sort of wait-and-see really. You know, Tommy's going to be a very tough opponent. Come Thursday, I'm going to have to be, you know, playing my best tennis if I'm going to get over him. You know, there's certainly a little bit of concern I think. But, you know, I've been able to get through a five-set match out there tonight against Jonas Bjorkman.

Q. You're a definite starter against Tommy?

LLEYTON HEWITT: Oh, yeah. At this stage, mate. I am going to get as much treatment. This is the Australian Open, this is a Grand Slam. Davis Cup and Grand Slams, that's what you live for as a tennis player. For me, playing in Australia, it's my favorite, you know, tournament of the year and, you know, I'm going to go out there and, you know, try and give it everything I've got.

Q. Must have been great having that sort of crowd behind you after what you went through in Barcelona. We were pretty much the exact opposite?

LLEYTON HEWITT: Yeah, the crowd was fantastic. You know, they lifted with me out there tonight, and, you know, I was two-sets-to-one down in that Costa match in the first rubber of the Davis Cup, and it sort of brought back a few memories when I was two-sets-to-one down in tonight's match as well. The energy that I could draw off the crowd tonight, you know, it was fantastic. It was unbelievable.

Q. Do you feel you can reverse it against Tommy? You mentioned as you came off the court you felt you'd be better prepared this time because you didn't have much practice going into Adelaide.

LLEYTON HEWITT: Yeah, Adelaide was really a warm-up week for me this year. I didn't give myself a chance of winning that title at all this year just because, you know, it was such a long and demanding year both physically and mentally last year. I didn't get to finish until a couple of weeks before Adelaide started. I didn't know until two days before the tournament whether I was going to play or not, so I really had very limited practice and preparation going into that tournament. I started to find some rhythm in Sydney, which is good, and just try to keep the ball rolling basically now.

Q. Congratulations for your big victory. You are a big fighter. When you were playing, what did you feel knowing that Rod Laver was in the public and watching you? Did you feel more energy?

LLEYTON HEWITT: With the crowd or...?

Q. Yes. Knowing that Rod Laver was in the public.

LLEYTON HEWITT: Rod Laver, oh.

Q. Did you feel something?

LLEYTON HEWITT: Yeah, it's fantastic. I got the opportunity to, you know, hit with Rod a couple of days ago in the charity day here on Vodafone Stadium over there. It was just, you know, a privilege being out there with, you know, possibly the greatest player of all time. You know, he's an Australian hero, he's an Australian champion, and unfortunately I never got to see him play. But by all remarks, he was an unbelievable player. It was fantastic to hit a few balls. For him to be out there, I'm playing in his arena, it's the Rod Laver Arena out there, for him to be sitting front row with all the Tennis Australia people, even Goolagong was there as well, it gives you a little bit of a lift I suppose.

Q. Did you think you were gone at any stage?

LLEYTON HEWITT: I never thought I was gone. I was definitely struggling out there, especially when I was two-sets-to-one down. It was a pretty big turnaround after I was a set and break up in that game. I held, then got broken.

Q. How do you keep yourself going? How do you keep yourself in a match?

LLEYTON HEWITT: It's hard. You got to draw on something in your will, in your body. You got to stay positive out there. That's the main thing. Once you start believing that you're beaten, then you are beaten. You know, in any of my matches, I never believe that I'm beaten until, you know, you shake your hands at the net. You know, it was just, tonight there was a lot of things that I could draw from. It was the crowd out there. It was, you know, just the feeling, you know, I had all my family and supporters in the crowd as well. You know, Wazza and some of the fanatics who followed us at Davis Cup there and the other section of the crowd. There's a lot of positive energy and vibes I could draw from out there. They helped me get over the line.

Q. (Inaudible)?

LLEYTON HEWITT: Yeah, it was very strange. I think Jonas gave all his tickets to the guys who paint their faces.

Q. Lleyton, considering the hamstring problem and the fact that you were down two-sets-to-one, how would you rate this week compared to some of your other better wins?

LLEYTON HEWITT: It's, the way -- you can't really look at it. The way I hit the ball was fantastic out there tonight. Obviously I had to deal with a few problems out there. But for determination and guts, it's definitely up there with, you know, it's equal to the Davis Cup thing, Davis Cup match against Costa. You know, that match was for your country. It's probably a little bit bigger, but this is right behind it I think out there tonight.

Q. After this win, the crowd, do you rate yourself favorite against Tommy?

LLEYTON HEWITT: As I said, it's probably even I'd say. You know, last time Tommy beat me in Adelaide, time before that was in Miami earlier last year where I actually, you know, beat him pretty convincingly in that match. So, you know, I feel like it's probably a pretty even match. Tommy sort of struggled there for probably about a year. After he started doing well, he beat me here a few years ago actually in the second round and went on to make the semifinals.

Q. Is he a special player for you?

LLEYTON HEWITT: Well, I think he's a very good player. I think he's, you know, he's going to be in the Top 10 very shortly. You know, I think he's a hell of a player.

Q. Did you plan to come to Italy this year for the Italian Open?

LLEYTON HEWITT: Rome again? Yeah, well it's a Masters Series event, so, yeah. It's in my schedule at the moment. I played well there last year. I made the semifinals there, so I enjoyed playing.

Q. We look forward to you coming to Italy.

LLEYTON HEWITT: I hope the crowd's on my side.

Q. How about the Swedish crowd?

LLEYTON HEWITT: They're very loud. I've been coming to the Australian Open for years and, you know, I used to idolize Stefan Edberg and Mats Wilander. You know, something that other players have to deal with when you're playing a Swede. I think it's good for the Australian Open. They're always there with their faces painted and their bodies painted and yelling out each side to each other. I think it's good for tennis. Obviously tonight it was sort of -- I had the rest of the crowd on my side, so I was very happy. They're very vocal for a small group of Swedes I suppose.

Q. You were throwing some glances at them a couple of times?

LLEYTON HEWITT: Pardon?

Q. You were watching them a couple times. Were you ever disturbed?

LLEYTON HEWITT: No. I never really focused on them at all during the match. You know, maybe I looked at it -- I was looking over toward my coaching group which was sitting close to them. I never really -- I block them out as much as possible.

Lleyton Hewitt Interview after beating Tommy Haas in straight sets in the second round at 2001 Australian Open.

THE MODERATOR: First question for Lleyton, please.

Q. Vicenzo Martucci. When do you think about the first set, when you was down 5-love, then went up. What do you think what happened with his mind, his style?

LLEYTON HEWITT: Well, for sure I think we're both saying probably thinking about the second set. I'm sure in his mind he thought with the opportunity of serving twice for the set that, you know, the set was his especially the way that he was playing. You know, he probably relaxed a little bit as well and I felt like after I broke him that first time, if I could, you know, I held off a couple of break points at 5-2, if I got out of that game I could have a crack at him. After you drop your serve once serving for the set you're nervous the second time. I think that's what happened. Then I started getting on a bit of a roll. He played another very order game at 5-all, his serve, give me that opportunity to serve for the set.

Q. John Parsons, The Daily Telegraph. Also do you think the fact that he got off, he did get off to a wonderful start, was playing great tennis, but did you have to build yourself mentally after that long match the other night? You needed time?

LLEYTON HEWITT: A little bit. I didn't come out with all guns firing I think. You have to take your hat off to him. He came out, hardly missed a first serve his first two or three service games. He was blasting me off the court at the start. Wasn't a lot I could do. I couldn't get any rhythm on my ground strokes out there. I didn't come out serve as well as I should have also. I gave him a lot of opportunities to get on top of my second serve early. Once I started getting confidence and moving the ball around more, I felt my forehand came in very handy today.

Q. How is your hamstring? Any problems physically today?

LLEYTON HEWITT: No, it was pretty good actually. Better than I thought it was going to be.

Q. You said you weren't quite 100 percent still but you sort of feel like you're getting closer?

LLEYTON HEWITT: Yeah, I think with, you know, every day that goes by I'm going to be a lot better for it. You know, I was very happy, you know, just to get through the last couple of matches with it.

Q. Does it feel like one of the hardest straight sets victories you've ever had?

LLEYTON HEWITT: Yeah, for sure. I just about felt like I was going to lose it. I was playing catchup tennis the whole day. To my credit, I just hanging in there, kept fighting, got the breaks when I needed to and played the big points well. Again, the third set I think he was starting to hurt a little bit out there. It was quite a long match for three sets. I think it was well over three hours. So I -- physically, it was probably a little bit more draining than a normal three-set match.

Q. Why is it that these circumstances bring out the best in you so often do you think?

LLEYTON HEWITT: It's hard to say. You know, I just -- I just get a buzz from walking around this place. You know, I've been coming to this tournament ever since the first time I played here at Melbourne Park I was playing here, I was just a young kid out in the crowd getting everyone's autographs. As soon as I, you know, got the opportunity to play Juniors here and, you know, it was just a dream come true to be playing here. And, you know, I remember watching Rochey and Lendl sort of warm-up at 9 o'clock out there on the courts, I used to be watching them. Now to be in that position out there playing, and, you know, me growing up on rebound ace as well, I feel so much at home out there at the moment.

Q. Ubaldo Scanagatta, La Nazione, Italy. Do you think that Haas has some problems when he has to finalize a match? I mean, he hit some lapse of concentration apparently.

LLEYTON HEWITT: Yeah, I haven't noticed it in the past. If you're just going to take it from today's match, sure, maybe he had a couple of concentration lapse when he got the break in each set. But, you know, in the past I haven't noticed that he's had a big problem in that area. I wouldn't say -- I think it's just one match that happened to him today. Obviously he's going to be very disappointed when he looks back on the match and sees that he had an opportunity in each set to really win each set out there today. But I don't think he's got a problem, you know, through his career with that.

Q. How do you feel about playing Carlos Moya next?

LLEYTON HEWITT: You know, obviously the draw doesn't get any easier, that's for sure. I'm going to have my work cut out again. I'm going to go out there, play the way that I've been playing. I can draw a lot of confidence that, you know, I've beaten two class players in the first two rounds. You know, I know he's beaten two very good players as well. Hopefully it's going to be a very good match but I'm expecting a very tough, long, sort of slugging out there. It's going to be a baseline match pretty much.

Q. How much has seven hours of tennis taken out of you in three days?

LLEYTON HEWITT: I actually feel, you know, pretty good. I feel a lot better than I did in Spain on the clay. It's probably because clay is a much more, you know, sort of physical, physical surface rather than rebound ace. To play out there, it was pretty hot out there on center court today on the rebound ace. I'm feeling pretty good at the moment. I was surprised how well I felt apart from the hamstring after my match against Bjorkman.

Q. How much did the crowd help you out there, being in Australia? How much of a spur was that when you were love-5 down in that first set?

LLEYTON HEWITT: Yeah, I knew that if I could get things going, the crowd was going to hop on as soon as I got it going. That's the big, you know, that's a huge advantage for the Australian players. We saw Andrew Ilie yesterday, Pat Rafter every time he comes out to play, Wayne Arthurs. It's a huge lift for the Australians, as soon as we get that edge or we get that opportunity to break serve and get up a break, the crowd's really on us. It's very good to, you know, it's very easy for us out there as well to work with the crowd and get positive vibes from the crowd as well. That's something that, you know, I've learned to do I think pretty well over the last couple of years.

Q. Do you feel you can get through two weeks of the tennis you've been playing so far, play the mix doubles as well?

LLEYTON HEWITT: It's hard to say at the moment. Obviously the singles is the priority. You know, I've just been taking it one match at a time. Obviously the first two matches have been very hard-fought matches. Hopefully they get a little bit easier somewhere along the line. I've got to be prepared to play seven matches in singles, you know, five sets if you're going to win the tournament. So, you know, that's something that I knew coming into the tournament and that's something that I sort of planned my -- to be peaking sort of for this time of the year.

Q. Does it annoy you that your interaction with the crowd in your case actually draws a lot of adverse comment both from fans and from the media?

LLEYTON HEWITT: Yeah, you know, I haven't heard too many bad reports from the fans. That's for sure. You know, the last three weeks has been, you know, a dream walking out on the court, as I said, you know, after just about all my matches, there's only, you know, just over a month ago we were in Barcelona I was getting booed by 14,000 people. As I said, I can't say how, you know, words can't describe how much of an advantage it is to have 15,000 people, you know, screaming for you, behind you. And I've been fortunate enough the last three weeks that everyone's been behind me. It was fantastic in Adelaide. Sydney was great as well, very big stadium there. The last two matches here, I think we've seen how the crowd's responded to me out there and, you know, they're one of the main reasons why I got through that match against Bjorkman, that's for sure.

Q. Doesn't worry you when you're criticized in the

media?

LLEYTON HEWITT: No. I think the fans know what's going on and, you know, I know what's going on and that's all that matters.

Q. This same fact that the crowd is behind you doesn't create a lot of pressure, and you know they are expecting you to win a Grand Slam?

LLEYTON HEWITT: I don't know if they're expecting me to win. I've never made it to a final of a Grand Slam. You know, but I think, you know, I don't feel any added pressure when I go out there because the crowd's behind me. You know obviously they want to see the Australians do well and it's something that Pat's probably had to deal with the last few years as well. He hasn't always performed well in Australia. Obviously the last few years with Davis Cup ties and that he's doing better and better. I was lucky enough, this is -- it feels like, you know, just coming home really and playing because this is where it all started for me, Adelaide, Sydney and Melbourne. Started my career and it really does feel like sort of I'm out playing in my backyard out there. So I don't put any added pressure on myself, you know, what the spectators think I should be, winning or losing.

Q. Talking about Barcelona. What did the King of Spain said to you when you finished the match against Ferrero?

LLEYTON HEWITT: He just said, "Great match and good fighting," you know, it was fantastic to watch.

Q. He was quite nice?

LLEYTON HEWITT: He was very nice.

Q. In your personal rankings, this match you are playing, they are very, very tough. How do you think is this matchup today? Which level? Second, third?

LLEYTON HEWITT: I don't --.

Q. The tougher matches you've played?

LLEYTON HEWITT: Tough matches, Tommy's a very tough player to play against. I can't see any reason why he's not going to be in the Top 10 for the next, you know, five to ten years. I think he's a fantastic player. He's got every shot in the game. When he's on, he's very hard to beat as I found out in Adelaide. So I rate him as an opponent very tough. So, you know, definitely up there with one of my toughest matches.

Q. Yes, but was tougher with Bjorkman or today?

LLEYTON HEWITT: It's hard to say because they play totally different. Bjorkman tried to rush me a lot more than Tommy did out there today. Tommy's a more free flying baseliner, he serves a lot bigger. Both matches were equally as tough. I could have lost three sets to love out there against Tommy, whereas Jonas I was pretty much in the match even though I was down two sets to one.

Q. Could I just ask you if you happen to be drawing up a betting market on -- if you were to be a betting man, I don't know, how many players would be in front of you? Would it be four? Two? Six? What?

LLEYTON HEWITT: Definitely be all the Grand Slam winners. You know, I think when it comes down to experience, those guys who have won the Grand Slams before, whether it's Rafter, Agassi, Sampras, Kafelnikov, Safin, Kuerten, I don't know if I've missed anyone, I think they should all be above me just because I haven't been in a Grand Slam final before. You know obviously there's going to be a time when hopefully I get that opportunity to walk out there on the, you know, on the Sunday, the last Sunday of a Grand Slam. But at the moment, I think they've got to be, you know, the favorites ahead of me.

Q. How do you feel about tennis people that have regards about you punching the air? Does that criticism from tennis people have more impact? Does it affect you at all?

LLEYTON HEWITT: No, I haven't heard too many tennis people, you know, -- I think it's more, you know, I don't think really anyone sort of in the tennis people have bagged me before.

Q. Someone said you went like this. (Inaudible) He said he was a bit upset by it. Does that have any impact?

LLEYTON HEWITT: No, I think the only time I got pumped when he did a double-fault was 4-2 in the fifth. I think everyone understands when you've been out there four hours, get a break in the fifth set, you're allowed to look over to your sidelines and give a fist pump.

Q. I think it was Tommy towards the end of the second set when he lunged for a volley and you won the point. He was down on the ground several seconds. How does it feel to see your opponent literally face down on the ground not moving? Must have been an invigorating sight?

LLEYTON HEWITT: Geez, that's hard to say. It's not like he was about to die out there, I can tell you that. I didn't actually -- I thought he was getting up pretty quickly. As soon as I turned my back, he was already up and he was ready to play on. Obviously if he goes for a dive volley he's going to end up on the ground. Otherwise, keep on your feet.

Q. When you were a kid, were there talks about your fist pumping? You're in the spotlight. Obviously that's what people are focusing on. Did anybody ever --?

LLEYTON HEWITT: Not really. I didn't, you know, I only do it at the times that I feel it's necessary. Whether that is getting a break in the fifth set or getting a break in the first set, when I feel like I needed to get myself pumped up on the court and give me a -- sort of a lift out there, that's what I do it for. And, you know, no one's really had a go at me coming up the junior ranks at all.

Lleyton Hewitt after losing to Carlos Moya in five sets in third round of 2001 Australian Open.

THE MODERATOR: First question, please.

Q. What do you think made the difference in the end? Is there one point or one difference between you two?

LLEYTON HEWITT: You know, it's hard to reflect on the match straight after it. You know, it was as close as anything, you know, whether it was getting the break point early in the fifth set was probably my big opportunity I think. You know, but then again, you know, if I could have held serve early in the second set after I won the first and really sort of got in a bit of a roll, a bit of rhythm, he was spraying balls early in the match. I gave him that confidence boost early in the second set, and he took full advantage of that.

Q. I mean it's just a hell of a difficult match to lose and to have to come in so soon after is probably difficult to sink in as well. Not an easy one for you, is it?

LLEYTON HEWITT: No.

Q. And all the circumstances?

LLEYTON HEWITT: No. At the end of the day, I gave everything I had. And, you know, in all three of my matches, I had to work my butt off the whole time. I didn't get too many, you know, cheap points against the three guys that I played. They're all very class, highly rated players. Obviously the draw didn't go my way, I suppose, and I didn't give myself a chance to work my way into the tournament. But there's nothing I can do about that. You know --.

Q. Do you think you suffered a little bit almost for the way you play? You get dragged into long matches. It's almost the way you are.

LLEYTON HEWITT: Yeah. You know, little bit. But I think still, you know, if I played three guys ranked 70, 80, 90 in the world, a qualifier, wildcard, then it could have been a totally different story I think. I drew a guy who's been No. 4 in the world, I drew a guy who's been No. 1 in the world and, I drew Tommy Haas, who I would have rated him probably before the tournament as the best unseeded player. I didn't get too kind in my section, but there's nothing I can do about that at all. You win some; you lose some.

Q. (Inaudible)?

LLEYTON HEWITT: Actually, I felt pretty good. Obviously, you know, I don't know how long it went, probably close to four hours in the end. But once it starts getting to that stage, it doesn't matter how, you know -- I'm sure Carlos is feeling it as well. Once you get into that long situation, deep in the fifth set, then you start feeling it for sure. You know, I felt pretty good for the first few sets out there. I was quite surprised, considering that, you know, I haven't done any fitness work or anything for the last four or five months. So, you know, I've got a good base to work on. That's what I'm trying to say.

Q. How do you see now the chances of Moya to go further in the championship?

LLEYTON HEWITT: Well, you know, I think it's open. A lot depends on how he pulls up, though, in two days' time. I give him a very good chance of doing well. Whether he can win it or not, that's another story because, you know, last year he really struggled, last year and a half I suppose. But he is a class player and, you know, as soon as he gets his confidence back and he starts working that forehand, he has a very good serve on him for a baseliner as well. So he's going to be very hard to beat.

Q. How great was the expectation you felt coming into this as Australia's sort of favorite chance here I guess? How much of it did you put on yourself?

LLEYTON HEWITT: I didn't put any on myself. I came in hoping that I was going to be hitting the ball well before I sort of came into the whole summer circuit, then, you know, I was very happy the way I played in Sydney and got myself in good condition after losing in Adelaide in the quarters there. But, you know, it was very hard to expect huge things, because, you know, before the Davis Cup I, in my mind, was worried I was going to play the Davis Cup final or play the Australian Open circuit. You know, my breathing was that bad at the time. Darren had sat me down and said, "You're probably going to have to miss one of these, which one are you going to miss." I took my chances in the Davis Cup, and as it turns out, I've taken my chances for the Australian Open circuit as well. I really didn't give myself the greatest chances, I think, of doing well in both situations due to, you know, things that I can't, you know, are out of my control anyway.

Q. You were prepared to miss this event to play Davis Cup?

LLEYTON HEWITT: That's what I did at the start, yeah. Davis Cup's my priority.

Q. Would it be fair to say that you would be pleased not to see any more Spanish players for a while?

LLEYTON HEWITT: I got nothing against Carlos at all. You know, he's --.

Q. Just sort of the circumstances of Ferrero in Barcelona and now this tonight, you could probably do the --?

LLEYTON HEWITT: Oh, I can definitely -- I don't want to keep coming off against them. But, you know, that wasn't in my mind going into the match at all. You know, Carlos had nothing to do with Barcelona at all.

Q. What now before Davis Cup?

LLEYTON HEWITT: Try to get my body right. You know, I'm struggling with my hamstring at the moment. That's the priority - to try to get that right in time because, you know, I've been taking a lot of tablets and stuff to try and get it right for these two weeks. Now I've really got to get off that and try and get it 100 percent for the Davis Cup tie, then the American hardcourt season.

Q. Are you feeling twice your age at this stage?

LLEYTON HEWITT: Yeah, it's unbelievable. I feel worse than Darren. He complains about his knees; I got worse things going on than him at the moment.

Q. Are you now looking to take a break for mental health reasons?

LLEYTON HEWITT: No, the schedule doesn't really allow me to take a break. You know, I've got a Davis Cup tie on grass which is going to take a bit of getting used to after playing on rebound ace, switching to grass. You know, this stage, I don't really have an opportunity to sort of lay out four or five weeks. That was the problem with the breathing thing. You know, they recommended having surgery and that. I couldn't really lay out a time that I'd be out for four or five weeks which I could, you know, take that time off and get it done properly and then come back on the circuit.

Q. If you don't take a break, aren't you worried that you'll be forced to take a break?

LLEYTON HEWITT: Not at the moment. My breathing's actually feeling a little bit better with the tablets I've been taking and the nasal spray. The hamstring, which happened practicing here a few days before the tournament started, that is a once off thing. If I can get that right before the Davis Cup tie, you know, I think I'm gonna be fine.

Q. There's no kind of situation where having to play as it were an indoor match affects you in any way, is there? Because clearly the air doesn't move around as

much.

LLEYTON HEWITT: Yeah, no, I feel pretty good out there. And in Barcelona I felt, you know, I'm definitely not normal, not 100 percent of what I've been in the past. But for the way that I've been going, I felt pretty good out there.

Q. Think Pat can win this event?

LLEYTON HEWITT: Yeah. You know, I think the way that Pat's been playing, I've only seen his few matches, two out of the three matches that he's played, but he seems to be hitting the ball well. I hit with him this morning actually. He's confident I think. He hasn't had a lot of pressure I think going into him as well. He's been able to sort of build his game up. You know, it's a big test for him tomorrow, I think, to play his first real name player in the tournament so far, round of 16. I think Henman's playing very well as well. So, you know, I take Pat to win, you know, because I know that he wants it, you know, as much as I do and every other Australian, Andrew Ilie or whoever.

Lleyton Hewitt Interview after winning 2001 U.S. Open vs. Pete Sampras 76 61 61.

MODERATOR: Questions for Lleyton.

Q. As a Grand Slam champion, you have to take your hat off.

LLEYTON HEWITT: Take my hat off? My hair's not done (laughter).

Q. Well done.

LLEYTON HEWITT: Thank you.

Q. You must be delighted with your performance today.

LLEYTON HEWITT: Yeah. It hasn't sunk in yet. You know, walking out there to play Pete Sampras in your first-ever Grand Slam final, it's, you know, something that you'll never forget, that's for sure. Obviously, I had a few nerves coming in there playing possibly the greatest player ever to live in probably my biggest ever match, you know, in tennis. I got off to a pretty good start, then got broken straight back. You know, just sort of settled the nerves. That was pretty good.

Q. You weren't awed, were you? You've been talking about your firmness of mind and how you can block things out, and you have blocked things out. I don't really believe you were awed out there. You just went right after him from the first game.

LLEYTON HEWITT: I've looked forward to this moment. You know, it's something that, you know, you dream of doing, walking out there and playing in a Grand Slam final, you know, playing that seventh match of two weeks. I didn't want to let the chance sort of slip by, that's for sure. I was definitely up for the match. I felt I'd been getting better and better each match that I played. You know, I definitely gave myself a big chance today, the way that I was hitting the ball, every second day got better.

Q. How crucial was that first tiebreak in terms of establishing some sort of psychological lead anyway?

LLEYTON HEWITT: Yeah, it was huge, no doubt about it. You know, I was under a fair bit of pressure on my service games throughout the first set. I was able, after dropping it in the second game, able to sneak out of those service games. It was pretty big. I started as well up the better end.

I started the tiebreak. I knew I had to get off to a pretty quick start, otherwise Pete was going to be on me in the second half of the breaker. Changed ends at 3-All after doing a double-fault. Still gave myself a pretty good chance, knowing I played a great passing shot at 4-3 to get the mini break. I was able to hold on from there.

Q. Was that better than Brazil or on par?

LLEYTON HEWITT: It's hard to say. I think they're two totally different situations. You know, Davis Cup, you're playing for your whole country. You're playing for your nation. You know, still I knew all the Australians were behind me when I went out there to play today, as well. I think it's on par with when I beat Kuerten in Brazil.

Q. Did you have any problems with the wind?

LLEYTON HEWITT: It was tough. It's one of the toughest condition days that I've had to play in and had to deal with. I felt like I got better and better. But early it was very tough because, you know, Pete hits the ball so heavy. He's got a big serve. I really didn't get too many chances up the end when he was serving with the wind. He didn't give me too many chances on most of those games. I was trying to fight my butt off to hold serve that first set up that first end. It was extremely tough in that sense. Then I started passing well after that.

Q. Did you watch the US Open final last year and see how Marat handled Pete? Did you ever think, "I might be able to do that someday"?

LLEYTON HEWITT: I watched probably a set I think before leaving. I was out of here. But, you know, Marat handled himself great in his first Grand Slam final, as well. You know, I just knew, believing in myself, that I was capable of doing it out there, handling the pressures that come with going into your first Grand Slam final. You know, I've been through a lot of things for a 20-year-old, and I've played a lot of big matches, especially in Davis Cup ties. I've come out of those, you know, pretty well so far.

Q. Were you nervous last night? Were you thinking about the match? Did you sleep well?

LLEYTON HEWITT: Yeah, I was nervous. You're not human if you're not going to be nervous going into your first Grand Slam final, but I'm sure any Grand Slam final you'll be nervous. It was very hard to sort of eat too much, as well. I didn't really feel like eating this morning or even having a bit of lunch and stuff today. You know, it was probably the fact that you have to play Pete Sampras in your first Grand Slam final as well. There would be a lot of easier guys to play. You know, he's a big match player.

Q. Has the aura of Pete Sampras now changed with his two losses in the finals?

LLEYTON HEWITT: Not at all. You know, he's a great champion. I think, you know, when everyone was starting to write him off, especially after he lost in the Round of 16 to Federer at Wimbledon, I think he's come out and proved a point over the last two weeks. He's capable of winning Grand Slams still, that's for sure. You know, I've still got as much respect for him as a player, on and off the court, you know, as I've ever had.

Q. You said last night that you were going to ask Patrick for some tips. Did you end up doing that?

LLEYTON HEWITT: I spoke to Pat, yeah.

Q. Did he give you any tips?

LLEYTON HEWITT: He told me go out there and enjoy myself. That's all he told me. He said he felt exactly the same way as I felt, you know, going in the night before he had to play a Grand Slam final, him a few years ago. He said that Newk and Roche had told him in the past, he asked, "What do I do now?" He just said, "Go out and enjoy yourself." I asked him the same thing, and he told me exactly that. I tried to take that into my match today. In the back of your head, you're still thinking it's a Grand Slam final out there you're about to play.

Q. How is this going to change your life? How do you think it's going to change you when you go into Grand Slams in the future?

LLEYTON HEWITT: Don't know. Haven't even thought about it (laughter). You know, I'm still going to be the same person. I'm going to go home, I'm going to hang out with my mates, then I'm going to prepare for a Davis Cup tie in two weeks' time. It's not going to change anything in that way. But, you know, it hasn't quite sunk in. It's an unbelievable feeling to have won a Grand Slam now. You know, it probably takes a lot of the pressure and expectation off your back, as well.

Q. You're not old enough to have a beer here. Is that going to be a problem?

LLEYTON HEWITT: I don't know (laughter). You know, it hurts when back in Australia I can have one a couple of years ago, and I can't still have one here, so...

Q. Other than the winning point, what was the biggest point for you?

LLEYTON HEWITT: You know, probably the passing shot that I hit at 4-3 in the breaker to get that mini break up. I think that first set was pretty crucial. I felt if I could get that first set and try and get on top of him, I had a lot better chance than if I lost the first set.

Q. What is it about your personality that allows you to block out the distractions, the pressures?

LLEYTON HEWITT: Don't know. Got no idea. You know, I just grown up doing it, I think. It's something that I've had to deal with growing up in the Juniors back home in Adelaide when I was playing against older guys. You know, I was No. 1 in Australia a couple years out of my age. Everyone was out to beat you back then. I had to deal with those pressures and I had to be very mentally tough. I've been able to take that. I've got stronger in the head as I've got older, as well, I think.

Q. Marat last year just seemed so stunned with his own performance. He described it as an out-of-body experience. Looking back, he can't believe that was him on the court. With you, it seems like this is sort of almost a natural progression. Do you recognize the guy that was out there?

LLEYTON HEWITT: You know, a little bit. It's come in stages, which has helped, that's for sure. I first came on the tour, you know, I qualified for the Australian Open. That was a big shock then. Sort of gradually built up higher and higher. My ranking has gone higher and higher each year. After this, I'll probably be No. 3 in the world. It's career best. You know, that's been a good thing. I haven't been sort of having those highs and lows all the time. I've been gradually getting better and better. You know, the results that I've had in some of those big matches has definitely helped me in big matches in Grand Slams, I think. You know, there's no doubt that in my mind beating Guga in straight sets in Brazil was, you know, I could not have hit the ball any better out there. And that gives me the confidence in big matches when everything's against you, to go out there and do it in times like today, you know, the last three or four days when I've had, you know, pretty tough guys to come up against.

Q. Did you get any advice from Kim before the match?

LLEYTON HEWITT: Go and enjoy myself. That was basically it. She'd been through a lot. She knew it was a big occasion. Obviously, she came so close, two points away from the French Open. She knows what it's like to be in that situation. I can tell you it's a lot easier being out there playing instead of sitting in the crowd and watching that French Open in Paris.

Q. Pete called you the best returner in the game. What do you think about that?

LLEYTON HEWITT: That's a big compliment. You know, return of serve is one of my strengths, that's for sure. But, you know, I've had to work on little areas of my game because I don't have the biggest game, you know, with the serve. I'm not the tallest and strongest guy out there. So I've had to work on little areas of my game to sort of be able to counter-punch those bigger guys. The return of serve has been something I've had to work on since I was 9 or 10 playing in four- or three-year age groups playing the bigger guys. I've always been a big returner of serve. You know, to be the best in the world, that's a big call though, when you have especially guys like Andre Agassi. I rate him the best in the world.

Q. It's been a long time since an Australian has won the Australian Open. Quite a while since an Australian has won at Wimbledon. You guys come in here and won three of the last five. What's the deal?

LLEYTON HEWITT: I got no idea. It's strange. It really is strange. When I first came on the tour, if anyone told me where I was going to win my first one, I would have predicted the Australian Open just because I've grown up there, I always play well in Australia. You know, hard court is very similar here, as well. I try to take that same confidence, you know, growing up on hard courts, into here. It's very easy when I get in pressure situations, I know what to do on hard courts. These courts are pretty similar to the ones in Australia.

Q. Maybe a little less pressure here?

LLEYTON HEWITT: Yeah, I don't know. I haven't really -- I don't think I've, you know, lost in Australia because of pressure. You know, I lost this year because I had a very tough draw. I played a lot of matches going in probably, whereas the last two years when I've done well here, I've had a week off before, both Slams here. Maybe that's a thing I have to look at going into the Australian Open.

Q. You say it hasn't sunk in yet. Watching you when you lifted your trophy over-the-head, I wonder if the sense of the occasion really hit you then. What was going through your mind?

LLEYTON HEWITT: I looked at the names on the trophy, it was sitting in front of me. To see the guys who have held up this trophy, to now have my name under those guys', it's an unbelievable feeling. It's something words can't describe. You dream of winning a Grand Slam, you know, when you're a young boy sort of looking up. I've been to so many Australian Opens, watched so many great players win there. You know, it's these moments you dream of. For me, you know, to come through at such a young age, it's fantastic.

Q. Who were your greatest heroes in Australian tennis?

LLEYTON HEWITT: Australian tennis? You know, it was a strange sort of time when I was growing up. Pat Cash was sort of really the only guy when I was growing up. I was pretty much about on the tour when Pat started to win the Slams. Pat Cash obviously. Just for a guy to sort of idolize.

Q. Other players?

LLEYTON HEWITT: I loved watching Mats Wilander play, no doubt about that. He plays a similar game to me, as well. I love Stefan Edberg as well. For some reason, two Swedes, I like them.

Q. What kind of messages of support did you get from Australia before the match?

LLEYTON HEWITT: I got a couple of faxes the last couple weeks from John Howe. Starting at the top, that was pretty impressive. That meant a lot to me anyway. From my football team, that was all right, especially after their loss on the weekend. Everything has been very positive from all the fans back home, through my mates that I used to go to school with and I'm very close to and speak to every day. You know, they've sent their best wishes. Everyone who I know back in Adelaide.

Q. You have something of a mixed popularity amongst the Australian public since you came on the scene. Are you hoping now this sort of silences your critics, that

everyone will embrace you more now?

LLEYTON HEWITT: You know, it would be great. You know, I love playing in front of my Australian fans, no doubt about that. I can't wait for two weeks' time to get back there and play in Sydney. You know, I'm sure that everyone in Australia was fully behind me today. That's the type of country we are. We love, you know, supporting top athletes, you know, seeing another countryperson in a final. It's like other guys, me watching the cricketers, stuff like that, the rugby. I'm sure everyone was behind me back home.

Q. Throughout sporting history, there have been figures with great talent. Also some have had a fiery personality. They've spent practically all of their careers listening to people tell them they should behave this way, that way, don't do this, do that. You almost fall into that category now. You've come through it all magnificently. Do you think any of this will ever change you, or do you think it's something you'll decide whether you're going to be different in a match or with a crowd?

LLEYTON HEWITT: Oh, I go out there and I get pumped up on a court when I feel like it's necessary to get pumped up. You know, the last three or four matches, I really haven't showed that much emotion out on the court. It's been some of my biggest wins out there. You know, I've had to learn how to play best-of-five-set matches, as well. It's a lot different when you come on the tour, get very pumped up after each point out there. It's only in a three-set match where it's totally different. When you get to the Grand Slams, you can waste some of that energy on not the right points. That's something I've had to work on. It's been getting better and better I think with every Slam that I sort of play in that way. You know, I still feel, you know, like today when I won the first set, I felt that was a big occasion. I needed to get myself pumped up. I needed to sort of get my supporters behind me at that point because it was, you know, a pretty big turning point, getting first-set tiebreak. I feel like when it's necessary for me to get myself pumped up and play my best tennis, you know, that's when it comes out.

Q. Match point, you fell to the ground. You got up and were almost subdued as you went to the net. Was that out of reverence to Pete, or was it a little bit of pity for him?

LLEYTON HEWITT: It's more no one likes to lose, I'm sure, Grand Slam finals, even though I haven't experienced it. The sort of shock of winning a Grand Slam sort of sent me on my back, on the floor. You sort of realize, "I've got to go and shake Pete's hand." That was pretty much it. A sign of sort of respect, I think.

Q. You've had obviously expectations throughout your career. You talked before about the methodical progression of your game to this point. Is it still a bit surreal to be sitting here in front of a final press conference at this tournament?

LLEYTON HEWITT: It is. I can't believe I'm sitting here. I don't know when it will sink in, if it ever will. I hope so. You know, just to have won a Grand Slam now, at the age of 20, four years ago I was here playing Juniors. I lost in the Round of 16 or something. My badge, I still have the junior photo on the front of my badge here. It wasn't that long ago when I didn't talk to any of you guys. No one was out there watching. I was playing Taylor Dent out here a few years ago, and no one could care less. Now in front of everyone, I have the world's TV cameras on me, in front of me. I went and told Kim, "I'm not going to wake up, this isn't going to happen." It is unbelievable at the moment. I'm sure that's what sort of Marat felt at the moment, as well.

Q. To have done it against Pete.

LLEYTON HEWITT: That's what I said. I'm standing there about to collect the trophy and hold up the trophy. I'm standing there and Pete's there holding up the runners-up plate. It just didn't quite click for me (laughter). But, you know, if there's ever anyone that, you know, you'd want to play in a Grand Slam final, if you were going to win, it was one of the greatest players ever to live.

Q. Was there a moment when you thought you were thoroughly in control of the match, not just ahead?

LLEYTON HEWITT: No, not really. You know, you're trying to block it out as much as possible that you could be winning the tournament here in such a big event. I really wasn't thinking. I even had to look up at the score board a couple of times just to check what the score was. "Is this really two points from the match here?" Really hasn't sunk in that I was that far ahead. I was still taking it one point at a time, one game at a time.

Q. You had the first break of 87 games of Pete's service. You broke him, after 87 consecutive games.

LLEYTON HEWITT: I knew he hadn't lost a lot of service games in the whole tournament. He had this incredible roll going on his serve. You know, it was important to try and get out of the blocks quickly. You know, if he gets ahead, he's going to try and bury you, that's for sure. He's that kind of player. If he gets on a serving roll, he's going to be tough to break. It was important to try to get an early break, but then I gave it straight back the next game. It was a bit of a dogfight to try to get out of that first set.

Q. To some extent, now that you just won this, your life is going to be turned upside down. Everybody is going to want a piece of you, offers to show up everywhere. Who are the people in your life that you would take advice from? Would it be Patrick Rafter, the older generation? Is it your family? Is it your coach?

LLEYTON HEWITT: Well, it will be a lot of those. Obviously my coach and my family. Then, you know, Pat, because he's been there and done that. He knows what it's all about. He's really taken me under his wing ever since I came on the tour, helped me out a lot. You know, I owe a hell of a lot to him, you know, for me sitting here right now. He's helped me out. A lot of people wouldn't understand, "Why is he helping out this 15-year-old kid when he's playing all these big matches?" He helps out a lot of junior tennis in Australia. The other two are probably Newcombe and Roche. They're the two older guys that have been there and done that, as well, that I'm close to because of the Davis Cup. I owe them a lot, as well, for helping me out and taking me under their wing as well in the Davis Cup team.

Q. After the Blake match, did you learn anything from that incident?

LLEYTON HEWITT: Yeah, you know, it wasn't a good situation. It wasn't a good situation to put myself into during a Grand Slam tournament either. It's something that is going to be one of the toughest things that I had to block out during a tennis event. You know, I really have to be proud of myself for the way I've done that under, you know, so much pressure, so many people looking at you, I suppose. You know, to be able to do that at 20 years of age, it really shows how mentally tough I've been over the last couple of days.

Q. Is that the worst moment in your career?

LLEYTON HEWITT: It's one of the worst, yeah. You know, I didn't mean anything bad by it at all, and it all got blown up. I copped a lot of flak for it, for something I didn't mean at all. It's something I was obviously disappointed by because, you know, I knew I was really innocent in the whole thing. That's why I tried to block it out as much as possible and just concentrate on my tennis. You know, who knows, I just think I've done that really well over the last week or so.

Q. John Newcombe said that press conference for you last Friday must have been a nightmare for a 20-year-old. Was that a fair comment?

LLEYTON HEWITT: It wasn't too enjoyable. It's something that I'll learn from. You know, the media side, if I didn't deal with it properly or whatever, then I'll learn from that. You know, you've got to go through some rough times, as well, to become a better person and better player, on and off the court. If I had to go through it, you know, maybe I'll be stronger for it and, you know, maybe this is one of the signs of it.

Q. You said yesterday you were looking in terms of winning your first Grand Slam at 23 or 25. In view of this, what are your wishes now? What do you think your ambitions will be?

LLEYTON HEWITT: Got no idea (smiling). It's too early to say. You know, obviously I want to keep winning them. It's a good feeling. But it's not quite that easy. You've got to beat seven world-class players over five sets in two weeks to be able to hold up the trophy again. You know, it's going to be very tough. Obviously, going into the Australian Open next year, there's going to be a lot more expectation now coming off this win. I feel like it's a similar surface. I've played some big matches at the Australian Open. I'll be ready to go as soon as that starts.

Q. Did you have any idea that Paul McCartney was watching?

LLEYTON HEWITT: No clue. He was there?

Q. Yes.

LLEYTON HEWITT: Good (smiling).

Q. What are your thoughts on the upcoming Davis Cup?

LLEYTON HEWITT: You know, every time it gets close to Davis Cup ties, I get excited. For this whole tournament, I've had to try and block out that. The more I won, the later I was going to get to Sydney and start practicing on Rebound Ace and get ready for that. I've tried to block it out as much as possible. Tomorrow morning, that's pretty much one of the -- all I'll be thinking about is that Davis Cup tie, trying to get into another final. You know, the last two years in Davis Cup for me, ever since I started, my first tie was in Boston here in America. Ever since that, I love playing for my country and I love getting out there and competing. That's something that Newcombe and Roche and Patrick Rafter really helped me with. Obviously, it could be Pat's last year of playing Davis Cup matches. We didn't quite get over the line last year. We're sort of playing for Pat this year. I think that feeling came through in Brazil, the way I played, handled myself down there.

Q. How are you health-wise with this condition? Has it been affecting you at all?

LLEYTON HEWITT: It comes and goes. There's times when I could be out at dinner, and I feel like I'm short of breath. No one has a real, you know, reason for it. They're not sure if it's an allergy-related kind of thing. It's hard to put your finger on. You know, I've been feeling pretty good out on the court at least every time I've got to my matches, and I've been able to block it out. I definitely haven't been out of energy in any of my matches, which is a good thing.

Q. What do you plan for this evening? Taking a beer is not possible.

LLEYTON HEWITT: Got no idea. I'll definitely catch up with all of my friends and family who are here, have a nice dinner. Hopefully, you know, talk about the nice things that happened over the last two weeks, you know, what could happen maybe in the future.

Lleyton Hewitt after losing to Roger Federer in semifinal at 2002 Miami Masters Series 63 64.

THE MODERATOR: Questions for Lleyton.

Q. Two and a half hours last night. Little bit tired today coming out here?

LLEYTON HEWITT: Yeah, little bit. You know, I didn't -- I got off to a bad start as well, which probably hurt a little bit in the end. First game I had a few chances - 30-alls. Then, second game, I was up on my serve and lost it. If you can sort of get into the match, next game I had two break points to get back. Could have been easily up at least one break, you know, on my way. And it makes it a little bit easier from there. You go down straight a break straightaway, it's a long way home.

Q. Is it possible to be tired out there but not feel tired? Your muscles just aren't reacting as they normally do?

LLEYTON HEWITT: I don't know. You know, in Australia with the chicken pox and that, that was a case of thinking you had energy when you didn't. But, you know, that's a bit different, too, out there tonight.

Q. He hasn't been broken in this tournament yet. Can you just talk about how his serve has come along since the last couple times you faced him?

LLEYTON HEWITT: He's serving well, but I still had chances. I had a lot of 30-all games. As I said, I had a breakpoint -- few break points early in the first set in the third game. Then I had break points his first service game of the second set as well. So, you know, I had chances out there. You know, he's serving well and he's playing the big points well. In the end, if I played the big points well, could have been a different story.

Q. How do you look at him? He's very gifted; everybody knows that. Do you feel he can be a rival for you for No. 1 this year? Do you think he lacks some consistency?

LLEYTON HEWITT: I think he's getting more and more consistent every tournament. You know, he's had a pretty good start to this year, winning Sydney, playing a great match at the Australian Open, losing to Haas. Then, you know, at least making a final I think somewhere else as well. He's had a good start. I think this year could be a pretty big breakthrough year for him. Whether he's going to get up to top four or five, that's another question.

Q. Did you feel his presence at the net in the second set, in a sense that you changed the shots you wanted to go for?

LLEYTON HEWITT: I didn't think he came in, you know, heaps. You know, he volleys well. He's an all-court player. I didn't feel like I had to, you know, change my game though a lot to go for different shots than I normally would on the pass. I wasn't passing probably as well as I have in the past, but, you know -- in some other matches. But I don't think that was the time to sort of change what direction or how I was hitting the ball.

Q. Had that one volley right back at him in the second set giving him an easy pass?

LLEYTON HEWITT: That was me at the net though. So that's a bit different.

Q. It looked like, "This guy's been on the court way too many hours."

LLEYTON HEWITT: It's 50-50, he guessed the right way.

Q. How do you see the matchup in the finals?

LLEYTON HEWITT: Got no idea. You know, we'll let them work that out on Sunday.

Q. Next stop? Next stops?

LLEYTON HEWITT: Not sure yet. We'll wait and see. Probably Monte-Carlo though.

Q. What's on your mind clay-wise for Europe?

LLEYTON HEWITT: Yeah, I don't know. Still up in the air. So it's still up in the air. At this stage probably

Monte-Carlo's a chance. Apart from that, I really don't know.

Q. Do you want to play a lot of clay or very little?

LLEYTON HEWITT: Not heaps, but I definitely don't want to play too little either going in. I have to sort of try to find a happy medium there. Last year I played Rome, Hamburg, Dusseldorf. I felt pretty good, maybe I got a little bit tired towards the end of the French. So I will definitely be taking the week off before the French. That's different preparation than I've had going into the French before, so we'll see how that turns out.

Lleyton Hewitt Interview at 2004 Cincinnati Masters after first round match win against Alex Bogomolov Jr. 62 64.

Q. Is there something you're particularly trying to work on specifically in this tournament?

LLEYTON HEWITT: Not really. I guess just trying to get some match practice and get your confidence level up there in a big tournament against quality opposition going into the Grand Slam in a few weeks' time. If you're winning matches here, then you're obviously going to be confident going into New York.

Q. Can I ask you, just off the subject a bit, can you just think back to when you were with Darren. What did he bring to your game, what strong points did he bring as a coach when he was working with you?

LLEYTON HEWITT: You know, I guess at the start it was a little bit different 'cause I was, you know, I'd probably only been on tour for one year when Darren really took over. It was the end of '98, December '98. You know, I guess just for me, more than anything, I'd never really -- I was just traveling with my dad for that year, first year on tour. For me it was more having someone there who'd been through everything and, you know, the ins and outs of playing tennis, injuries. You know, he had a lot of experience, I guess, in that not as a coach on the tour but obviously as a player. I got along extremely well with him. We're both from the same state, and same city. You know, just overall I think he had a good presence.

Q. Do you think it was important to have a mate as well as a coach?

LLEYTON HEWITT: I think all the time for me it is. You know, tennis isn't like a football team where, you know, one coach has to look after 25 to 40 guys. You know, it's very one-on-one, and you've got to get along extremely well. He's got to be, you know -- for me and I'm sure most guys, you want to have a mate traveling with you because you spend so much time just the two of you.

Q. Just one more thing. When you got to No. 1, did your coaching needs change a bit vis-a-vis not about the split, but just in general, what you needed from a coach, what a coach could bring to you because he'd gotten you there?

LLEYTON HEWITT: Yeah, I don't know. I think there's things, you know, you can pick up from a lot of people, you know, little different areas that can help you. And there's no doubt that Stoltz brought a few different things to my game when he took over. You know, it was just some fresh ideas, I think, more than anything. I think that, you know, helped me out those two years that I worked with Jason. You know, I guess Roger, you know. I get along, I've been fortunate that I've got along with three coaches. They've been young guys who have been able to hit balls on the court. They have the same interest as me. I've got along extremely well with them.

Q. How close do you think you are to the kind of form that saw you reach No. 1 for two years in a row?

LLEYTON HEWITT: Yeah, I think there's been patches. Yeah, it's hard to say. There's been a couple of matches, I think, here and there. I think at Wimbledon, you know, right through the tournament I played pretty well. You know, it was no disgrace losing to Roger in the quarters. You know, I felt like it was probably, for me, probably the final out there that day and, you know, I went into the match like that. I think I handled the situation pretty well. You know, French Open, I felt like there was matches. Against Gaudio I didn't play my best tennis in the quarterfinals. But up till then I felt like I played as well as I probably ever played on clay through a whole, you know, tournament. I've had patches in the past when I was No. 1 that I'd have a good match here and there. So I think that was a big improvement this year even, even though I wasn't No. 1.

Q. Do you get more satisfaction from those kind of wins than perhaps you did towards the second year of being No. 1? Do you get more out of them because it's been a challenge to get to this point?

LLEYTON HEWITT: Not necessarily. I think, you know, on clay it's a little bit different probably. It's not my favorite surface, and it's something that I have to work extremely hard to get good results on clay, on that surface. This year, you know, it was rewarding. The guys I lost to, you know, in all the clay court tournaments were extremely good players and especially on that surface. I felt like I got better and better as the clay court season went on. I think that was rewarding. And hopefully that's gonna be, even though it's another 10-month break until I play on clay again, hopefully that's going to be a good stepping stone for next year.

Q. I guess it would help you coming into surfaces like this as well?

LLEYTON HEWITT: Yeah, I guess just having that confidence that playing on not your favorite surface and you're competing with the best guys in the world. So, yeah, definitely gives you -- it's very satisfying, I guess.

Q. This is somewhere where you've had very good results in the past. How confident are you of kind of taking the title here?

LLEYTON HEWITT: Oh, every match is tough. All these tournaments are the same. Indian Wells, Miami, Toronto and here are very similar tournaments. You've got to be able to win six matches in seven days against, you know, as tough an opponent as you're going to get in Grand Slams. I feel confident. I've played well here in the past - you know, except last year probably. I made a final and a semi. But, obviously, if I play Guga next, it's not an easy second-round match purely because I've got so much respect for his game and the kind of player he is as well.

Lleyton Hewitt interview at 2006 Indian Wells.

Q. How do you feel?

LLEYTON HEWITT: Not too bad. Be nicer if the weather was a bit warmer. But, no, it's pretty good. And yeah, it's one of my favorite tournaments. It's always nice to come back here and get stuck into it; the surface fits my game here. I've always felt very comfortable here. It's nice to come back to a place where you've played well in the past.

Q. How many of these tournaments did you play in California, like San Jose that you played before you came here?

LLEYTON HEWITT: How would you rate them or...

Q. Yeah, yeah, how do you rate your game?

LLEYTON HEWITT: Oh, my game, yeah, I feel like I got better and better, you know, after having three or four weeks off after the Aussie summer. It was a matter of trying to get as many matches under my belt as possible before coming in to these two tournaments, these two Master Series now, so I'm pretty happy to get ten tough matches under my belt and played some good tennis.
In the end, I started playing some better tennis and, yeah, I was pretty happy with how the body felt as well, which is definitely a positive.

Q. Is it harder year by year to prepare each year?

LLEYTON HEWITT: Not always. I guess I'm fortunate that in December and that, I can be in Australia and get acclimatized to conditions, and that's when you can -- you know, it's not a long preseason in getting ready, but, yeah, I can do as much as possible I guess before the Australian summer starts. So I'm definitely fortunate in that way. But, you know, you want to do enough work in November/December that you can just tough it out throughout the year 'cause you're not getting normally those seven-, eight-week gaps where you can actually do different stuff and work on your fitness and those kind of things. You've got to really last throughout the 11 months.

Q. Lleyton, what's your opinion of the instant replay, how it will affect your game?

LLEYTON HEWITT: I don't know. It's -- probably see how it turns out. I'm not sure whether it will be a huge positive or negative either way. It will be interesting, I think. If it gets the crowd involved a little bit more and stuff like that, it definitely can't hurt. Yeah, it's going to be different for officials, spectators, and players I think, so it will probably take a little bit of time for everyone to get used to.

Q. Have you played where they've used it?

LLEYTON HEWITT: No, I haven't, no.

Q. Are you concerned that it might disrupt the momentum of a match if someone's calling for them?

LLEYTON HEWITT: Yeah, well, there's definitely -- I think you have to have those couple of challenges, there had to be a limit on how many. You know, I think that's a good idea purely because you can't just keep going on every second ball so...

I don't think it should be too bad, you know. I've seen back home in cricket, you know, you have the third umpire for run-outs, stuff like that, yeah, it all happens pretty quickly.

Q. There really is no limit on how many if you keep making successful challenges--

LLEYTON HEWITT: If you make successful, yeah.
Q. So you can just go on forever?

LLEYTON HEWITT: Yeah, we'll see how good the players are, won't you.

Q. If you're accurate every time?

LLEYTON HEWITT: If you are, yeah, the umpire shouldn't be wrong that many times though, should they?

Q. What is your reaction to people that comment about your playing and going over the top and being an intimidating factor? Is that a component of your play, your energy you put out there or --

LLEYTON HEWITT: Just sort of happens naturally, I think, more than anything. You know, just the way I -- you know, I'm very competitive out there in whatever I do and in any situation.

So yeah, I think it's good to have a lot of different personalities out there and I think, you know, Nadal is very similar. We're both at very young ages, very hungry out there and want to succeed and want to get the best out of ourselves. And I think that's one reason why the two of us have been able to do it at such a young age as well.

Q. What changed in you like over the years? I mean, you were as young as Nadal and you were acting similarly as one might say, but what changed through the years? How do you see yourself now comparing to maybe five years ago when you were basically No. 1?

LLEYTON HEWITT: Not a whole heap, I don't think. Yeah, I think, you know, obviously, you're focusing from when you come on as a 16-, 17-year-old every week is like a Grand Slam, and, yeah, after you get to No. 1, you win a Grand Slam then the focuses and the priorities obviously change and Grand Slams and Davis Cup were my highest priorities. And that's what I was focusing on, you know, for three or four -- the last three or four or five years now. So it's basically you're working your schedule back. For me it's been working back to how I want to play my best tennis at what tournaments. Then I'll play as many tournaments that I feel I need before each of those to prepare as well as possible. But when you come on as a 15-, 16-year-old, you know, as I said everything -- every match is life and death out there as well where I think you see the bigger picture a lot more and looking after your body and trying to have as long a career as possible in this sport as well.

Q. I suppose after last year we ought to be asking how the toe is?

LLEYTON HEWITT: Yeah, it's good at the moment. It wasn't too pleasant playing, you know, the final last year the way I was feeling, but, yeah, something had to be done. It was needling me for far too long and, you know, straight after this tournament a year ago I went and had a small surgery. And yeah, it's feeling pretty good.

Q. Lleyton, after last week in Dubai you might consider Roger just that little bit beatable?

LLEYTON HEWITT: When Roger's played in big matches in big tournaments, you know, he hasn't put too many feet wrong. You know, obviously, last week -- I haven't seen a point of the tournament, but he was obviously, you know, in cruise control there for a little bit, 6-1, Love-30, and maybe lost concentration a little bit. And that's where you go back to Nadal's competitiveness out there. Yeah, he's got a never-say-die attitude. It obviously paid off for him last week. Yeah, whether Roger is a bit more vulnerable, we'll wait and see, but he's still the man to beat.

Q. Lleyton, does your agreement to play for Australia and Davis Cup signal a peaceful situation between you and Tennis Australia and consequently on the Australian Open on the courts?

LLEYTON HEWITT: It's always peaceful.

Q. How are you feeling then about the court at the Australian Open in changing the surface, because I

understand the TA is talking about it?

LLEYTON HEWITT: Well, I haven't spoken to them.

Q. How excited are you about the Davis Cup now that you've missed one?

LLEYTON HEWITT: It's good, yeah. The boys did extremely well over there, so, yeah, they've given us a good opportunity to get through to a semi again and you never know. If you get in the last four at the end of the year with home and away ties, you just never know how it's going to pan out. So, you know, I look forward to the opportunity, but Belarus isn't going to be easy whatsoever. They'll be some tough players and I think Myrni plays some of his best tennis in Davis Cup situations, so it's not going to be an easy tie for us. But, you know, I always love playing Davis Cup and look forward to the challenge yet again.

Q. Mark just said he's not available, 99 percent not available. Does that surprise you?

LLEYTON HEWITT: Yeah, but Mark's got to get -- you know, he's got to get more matches under his belt right at the moment. He's obviously had a sniggling back injury the last couple of weeks after playing a good match against Robredo in San Jose and, you know, I know he wasn't feeling great out there today on the court either. So, you know, I just think Mark's got to hopefully get some matches over the next few months and obviously just this Davis Cup tie come up after the first round pretty quickly, and if we can get through this one and Mark gets some good matches, especially on the grass, you never know. Maybe he'll be a contender for the semi finals in September.

Q. What do you reckon between Guccione and Luczak, say, based on what you saw in Geneva or heard about it?

LLEYTON HEWITT: Yeah, I don't know. It's totally different -- totally different match now as well. Different surface, different opponents. Either one of them, I'd feel confident with, but I've hit a lot of balls with both of them at different stages, and I think it's going to just depend on the week a little bit, who's hitting the ball where at the time. And Fitzy will make that call closer to the time.

Q. You sound sort of luke warm about instant replay. Would you do it differently than the way they've set it up or --

LLEYTON HEWITT: I'm not sure. You know, I haven't watched it close enough to tell whether, you know, it's going to be a major success or not. Yeah, only time will tell.

Q. Something in the sport you'd like to see happen, to change something in the sport?

LLEYTON HEWITT: Not off the top of my head right now. I think the game in itself is a lot of tradition, about, you know, the way we play the game, and, you know, the system and the scoring and all different things. And I think, you know, especially singles, I'd like to see it stay pretty much the same.

Lleyton Hewitt Interview after defeating James Blake 64 64 to win Queens Club in 2006.

Q. First title in a while. Must be pretty pleased that it's come here?

LLEYTON HEWITT: Oh, yeah, it's always nice to be playing on, you know, the last Sunday of a tournament, of any tournament. And, you know, this place has always been pretty special to me. You know, I really enjoy coming back here every year.
You know, sort of the same this year, I've got better as the week's gone on. And that's sort of been in the past as well when I've had to play Sampras and Henman and these guys in the semis and finals here, I've got better as the week's gone on. Hopefully, it's going to lead to good preparation for a week's time.

Q. What does this do for your Wimbledon confidence?

LLEYTON HEWITT: It doesn't hurt it, you know. I felt like in Paris I was hitting the ball well. It was a matter of trying to take that confidence after not playing a whole heap of tennis for a few weeks and sort of working, you know, getting confident on my ankle as well. And, you know, that's got better and better.
You know, I think once I started feeling like I could move a hundred percent out there, then it made life a lot easier for me to play my best tennis out there. And, you know, today, I felt like I played pretty flawless tennis for most of it. You know, I was pretty happy with the way that I struck the

ball. I served really well and put pressure on his serve as much as possible.

Q. When was the last time you felt in this sort of groove where it just seemed to click and you're feeling good about it and don't have to worry about the ankle or anything like that?

LLEYTON HEWITT: Uhm, it's hard to say, you know. Last year, it was a different year I guess because I sort of had these little periods where I had time off and I came here to London. I actually felt like at Wimbledon last year I was hitting the ball really well considering that I'd only played Queen's before that. I had a break from Indian Wells to Queen's through two different injuries.
Obviously, before that was sort of the Australian Open and Indian Wells, where I made both the finals there, and won Sydney. That was probably the last time that I actually was able to get on a bit of a run, I guess.

Q. As someone who's as competitive as you are, Lleyton, not having won your last four finals, was it beginning to get to you a little bit? Or you knew at some stage it would --

LLEYTON HEWITT: It was frustrating, you know, in terms of the finals that I've lost have, you know, all been, you know, tough matches. And, you know, against Murray it could have gone either way, six in the third. Against James in Las Vegas, I had chances early in the third set and ended up losing there, one break. Obviously, Safin in the final of the Aussie, and Federer in the final of Indian Wells. It hasn't been that I've played poorly in those finals, but if

you keep putting yourself in those situations, then
hopefully, you know, you're gonna come out on the right
side of it.
It's nice to win here, though, for a fourth time as well.

**Q. How much of a step up do you think you made today
compared with yesterday and the rest of the week?**

LLEYTON HEWITT: From my first match to today has
been a big step up. You know, I felt like, you know, I really
felt at home out there today on the court. You know, it was
pretty much, you know, the way that I've played in the past
here when I've beaten good grass court players. Yesterday I
felt like I was striking the ball well. It was a different kind
of match, I think. I had probably early chances in the
second set against Tim and wasn't quite able to take them.
But, you know, the way that I came out at the start against
Tim was similar to the way I played for both sets out there
today.

**Q. In this next week, this week off, what will you
concentrate on? Will there be anything specific that
you'll want to work on before the start?**

LLEYTON HEWITT: No, just sort of trying to keep the
rhythm there now more than anything. You know, as I said,
I felt like I was striking the ball well in Paris, especially in
my last two matches against Hrbaty and Nadal. It was a
matter of bringing that on to the grass, and I think I've been
able to, you know. Since adjusting from clay to grass, I
think the actual ball-striking has still been the same. Now I
just feel a lot more comfortable having five tough matches
on this surface. So it's a matter of just, I guess, keeping

your confidence up and, you know, staying relaxed and, you know, putting in enough time on there not to lose touch as well of the good things that I've done this week.

Q. Is this on a par, your form, with 2002, better or worse?

LLEYTON HEWITT: You know, the way I've played the last few matches, the last couple of matches anyway, I think ball-striking-wise, it's the same as when I won here, you know, the three times before. Um, you know, obviously, you know, Federer is going to be the guy to beat at Wimbledon. You know, who knows if I have to meet him in a quarter, semi, or final if I get there. But Grand Slams are funny things. You have to try to find a way to get through the first week and put yourself in a position in the second week, and a lot of strange things happen.

Q. Obviously, you don't lack confidence because you don't go on the court without that confidence, but how excited are you about the chance you've given yourself over the coming weeks now by this win, and the confidence boost you take with you?

LLEYTON HEWITT: Yeah, well, I feel confident. You know, I guess over the last year or so there's been times where I felt like I've hit the ball extremely well and, you know, I felt like I came awfully close to knocking Roger off in the semis of the US Open last year as well. There's been times where I just haven't been able to put a whole string of tournaments together, I guess, due to small niggling injuries. You know, this is obviously, you know, a small ankle injury going into the French wasn't the ideal preparation, but I feel like I've been able to turn that around now. Now it's heading in the right direction, so hopefully I can keep it going.

Q. Nice to share it on a -- you said on the interviews it's not Father's Day in Australia, but nice to share it with family?

LLEYTON HEWITT: Yeah, it's great. This is the first title I've obviously won since being married and having Mia. So, you know, it's nice to have them here with me, that's for sure. You know, apart from I guess winning a Grand Slam, this is probably the next best tournament, I think, for me.

Q. How does the field at Wimbledon stop Roger Federer this year?

LLEYTON HEWITT: I don't know. No one's been able to do it the last three years. So no one's really come that close either, I don't think. He's obviously had a few hiccups this week in Germany, but he still finds a way to win. That's why he's the best player in the world. It's gonna take someone to play an awfully good match, especially over five sets, to beat him at Wimbledon.

Q. Is there a preferable time to meet him in a tournament, semis, quarters?

LLEYTON HEWITT: No, not really. Up till the French Open, Roger had never lost, you know, a Grand Slam final before, so he's obviously extremely good in big matches, I think. You know, the last two years at Wimbledon I've lost to him in the quarters and the semis, so it would be nice for me to meet him maybe in the final.

Q. With the seedings for Wimbledon and the formula, first part of the question is do you agree that it is something different rather than just going with the rankings for the seedings? And where would you think you should be seeded? Roddick was saying yesterday that he doesn't see it as a shoo-in for him to be No. 2 when you consider Nadal's performance even though it's on a different surface. Looking at yourself, firstly, the formula then, where do you think you should be?

LLEYTON HEWITT: Obviously, you know, it's a bit strange last year to be No. 2 in the world and drop down after you've -- apart from Roger, I've been the last person to win the tournament. I find that a bit strange. I think that's probably the first time that something like that's happened, though. It's normally, you know, people that have done well or won the tournament move up, not down. So, for me, that was obviously a bit strange last year. You know, I wouldn't have a clue points-wise what the formula does or where it puts you or whatever. I wouldn't have the slightest idea.
So, you know, obviously, Roger and Nadal are that far ahead of anyone else in actual points that I find that - I don't know how it works - but I'd find it hard for Andy to catch Nadal. You know, I'm not sure how the point system works, though. But, yeah, Nadal is No. 2 for a reason, and, you know, he probably deserves to be the No. 2 seed, I think.

Q. Where do you think you should be?

LLEYTON HEWITT: No, I got no idea, mate.

Q. Are you following the soccer results?

LLEYTON HEWITT: Yeah, absolutely. You guys don't want to talk about the rugby, so talk about the soccer (laughing). You guys must be a bit worried about meeting us (smiling).

Lleyton Hewitt Interview at 2006 Wimbledon.

Q. Your comments about Agassi's announcement retiring later this year?

LLEYTON HEWITT: I just heard it five minutes ago, obviously he'll go down as one of the guys that changed our sport in many ways; not only the way he played the game, but the way that he conducted himself both on and off the court; the kind of character that he was for us as well. There's not too many more recognizable people out there, I think, in tennis. The sport probably owes a lot to him.

Q. What was your reaction to it when you first heard it?

LLEYTON HEWITT: Not that surprised, you know - was going to happen sooner or later. From what I understand, it is after the US Open, I think, seems like a pretty good place, obviously, after he made a great run there last year and he had had a lot of success there, so yeah, seems like a pretty fitting place to play your last tournament.

Q. Do you have any significant memories yourself; one

thing that stands out about Agassi's career?

LLEYTON HEWITT: One of the biggest weeks for me was my first tournament in Adelaide when I beat him. Not one of his best memories, I wouldn't think. For me, he was an idol growing up; a guy that I looked up to and especially playing on a grass surface as well, a guy that I drew a lot of confidence watching win Wimbledon and doing well here for so many years considering pressure from the back of the court; especially against Sampras and Ivanisevic and these kind of guys.

Q. After your chance at Queens, how are you feeling coming into Wimbledon and perhaps you can compare to the last two, three years since you last won the title, how good are you feeling right now?

LLEYTON HEWITT: I feel like I am hitting the ball well at the moment and it's hard going into Paris not 100% physically fit, but I felt like ball-striking-wise I was hitting the ball well, and yeah, I have tried to bring that same mentality into the grass court. I got better with every match. I felt a little bit rusty in the first match on grass, which is to be expected, but got better as the week went on.
By the end of it, I was playing some pretty good tennis out there. This last week has been a matter of just trying to keep that same rhythm going that I was able to do at Queens and trying to keep the confidence up there.

Q. Your thoughts on Volandri?

LLEYTON HEWITT: Never played against him. I wouldn't think grass is his favorite surface, but me out of anyone I think know that you can't take anyone lightly in this tournament. He's a talented base liner; has got good feel around the court; good hands. His serve, I wouldn't think is his biggest weapon. I will try to exploit it as much as possible.

Q. You have won Wimbledon. You know what it takes to win Wimbledon. What do you have to do to do it again this year?

LLEYTON HEWITT: I am not sure, you know, first week is a matter of getting through it and then, yeah, anything can happen in the second week. Obviously the last couple of years, yeah, I have come close in the quarters and semis. It was just one player was too good. It's a matter of trying to put yourself in that position again and giving yourself another crack at it.

Q. Is that one player still too good?

LLEYTON HEWITT: You have got to keep putting yourself in that position to find out. Yeah, it's going to take -- any person that's going to beat him in the next two weeks is going to have to play an extremely good match, and probably some of their best tennis.

Q. Having won it once, Lleyton, how sort of motivated and hungry are you to win it again? Perhaps having won it when you did, quite an early age as well, when you did, did it sort of go past you quickly? Would you like to have another crack at it and maybe absorb it a little bit more next time?

LLEYTON HEWITT: I think every time you come back

here you want to win it. Yeah, every time you walk in the gates, I think it is probably more special after you have performed well here; especially won here, you know, it's probably a more special place to walk into and, you know, the memories, I guess, come back a lot more when you have had good memories at any place. And this being one of the pinnacles of our sport, you want to try to put yourself in the position to be there on the last day, Final Sunday, but it's never easy.

Lleyton Hewitt interview after losing first round in Rome 2007 to Oscar Hernandez 63 67 61.

Q. Just what happened out there? Was it a matter of a rain delay, or are you feeling all right?

LLEYTON HEWITT: Yeah, a little bit. For the first two sets -- I felt like I was a better player the first two sets. I just didn't take my chances. Got off to a bad start in the first set and rain delay, courts play extremely heavy. Totally different conditions out there. He got better as the match went on. But, yeah, for the first set and a half, yeah, especially I felt like I was the one that had breakpoints and opportunities to go up a set and a break and perhaps serve for the second set, and I just couldn't take the breakpoints when I had them.

Q. Is it a bit frustrating to be always in the same sort of condition here in Rome, because this is not the first time this happened to you here?

LLEYTON HEWITT: Yeah. Last time I was here it was very similar. As I said, the conditions, when you come back out after a rain delay, are completely different. Yeah, the courts are a lot heavier and you're playing a lot slower than it was earlier.

Q. May I ask you, maybe it's an embarrassing question, but you have been No. 1 in the world 80 weeks, not just two or three. You play singles, and at the same time there is a doubles match where Nadal and Federer are playing and 4,000 people watch the doubles. What does that means to you? It's the media who have built up the image of those two top players right now and they don't give consideration enough to the other players? What's your reaction?

LLEYTON HEWITT: Well, those two, over the last two years or so, have been clearly the two best players in the world. You know, and I think considering -- yeah, apart from Roger's couple of losses to Canas this year, Nadal is the only guy that pushed Roger, especially on clay in the last couple years. I think everyone sort of looks forward to those matches because they know that Nadal has gone out there and had Roger's measure on clay. I think everyone knows that if Roger wins the French Open he can be the greatest player of all time. Yeah, obviously it's pretty intriguing at the moment when they get matched out there, and they don't play doubles that often. I wasn't here last year, but by all accounts they had a pretty epic match here. It's understandable the crowd is going watch them play.

Q. So it's not frustrating? You don't feel lonesome?

LLEYTON HEWITT: No, no, not at all. For me I only worry about going out there and playing my game and not worry about that at all.

Q. One more question about Kim Clijsters. Yesterday she decided to retire and she announce it officially. What was your opinion about that? It was a mistake to try to play this year when she had already planned to get married in July? She should have done something different, or what do you think?

LLEYTON HEWITT: Not necessarily. I think, you know, Kim's so well-liked around the world and she's played well in so many tournaments around the world that it would have been nice for her to compete for the rest of the year just for herself to get enjoyment, and obviously for the crowds as well. But I know how many injuries she's had over her whole career basically, and she's had to play through some tough times. She knows her body best. Everyone's -- very rarely do you walk on the court feeling 100 percent. So, you know, yeah, she's had a great career, though.

Q. For you now, where do you go now? Put a little wrench in your plans? French Open preparation?

LLEYTON HEWITT: Yeah, for me the French Open is the main goal on clay.

Q. Right.

LLEYTON HEWITT: Got two more tournaments: Hamburg and Austria before then. This week I was basically just coming here to try and get some matches and get in rhythm. I haven't played really since Indian Wells and Las Vegas basically. I was just feeling it out. You can practice on clay as much as you want at home, and we don't really have the caliber of players playing these tournaments.

Q. And for you, being Nadal and Federer are where they are, what is your goal? I mean, what is the goal of everybody more or less who was top, No. 1 in the world? To become No. 3? Or you still see the possibility or you dream about going back and being where you were?

LLEYTON HEWITT: Absolutely. You keep working hard and you keep working on areas of your game to improve. But, yeah, you don't really focus on Nadal and Federer that much. If you come across them, hopefully it's going to be later in the tournament anyway when you come up against them. Nine times out of ten those two guys over the last couple of years are the guys you got to beat to win Grand Slams. Obviously on clay Nadal is a stand out and on hard court and grass Roger's stand out. So yeah, it's always something that yeah, you try to improve your game every time you step at practice court. It's a lot easier said than done as well.

Chapter 5: Lleyton Hewitt's Two Seasons as ATP World No. 1

Lleyton Hewitt's Match Record for 2001

FRA V AUS F, Melbourne, Australia; 30.11.2001; DC;
Outdoor: Grass; Draw: 5

Round	Opponent	Ranking	Score
RR	Nicolas Escude (FRA)	27	L 6-4, 3-6, 6-3, 3-6, 4-6
RR	Sebastien Grosjean (FRA)	6	W 6-3, 6-2, 6-3

This Event Points: , ATP Ranking: 1, Prize Money: $

Tennis Masters Cup, Sydney, Australia; 12.11.2001; WC;
Indoor: Hard; Draw: 8

Round	Opponent	Ranking	Score
RR	Sebastien Grosjean (FRA)	7	W 3-6, 6-2, 6-3
RR	Andre Agassi (USA)	3	W 6-3, 6-4
RR	Patrick Rafter (AUS)	5	W 7-5, 6-2
S	Juan Carlos Ferrero (ESP)	4	W 6-4, 6-3
W	Sebastien Grosjean (FRA)	7	W 6-3, 6-3, 6-4

This Event Points: 750, ATP Ranking: 2, Prize Money:
$1,520,000

ATP Masters Series Paris, France; 29.10.2001; SU; Indoor:
Carpet; Draw: 48

Round	Opponent	Ranking		Score
R64	Bye	N/A	W	
R32	Nicolas Lapentti (ECU)		30	L 6-4, 4-6, 4-6

This Event Points: 5, ATP Ranking: 3, Prize Money: $17,500

ATP Masters Series Stuttgart, Germany; 15.10.2001; SU; Indoor: Hard; Draw: 48

Round	Opponent	Ranking		Score
R64	Bye	N/A	W	
R32	Bohdan Ulihrach (CZE)		33	W 3-6, 6-3, 6-4
R16	Guillermo Canas (ARG)		18	W 3-6, 6-1, 6-4
Q	Wayne Ferreira (RSA)	36		W 6-7(5), 6-3, 6-2
S	Tommy Haas (GER)	14		L 6-2, 3-6, 4-6

This Event Points: 225, ATP Ranking: 3, Prize Money: $120,000

Tokyo, Japan; 01.10.2001; CS; Outdoor: Hard; Draw: 56

Round	Opponent	Ranking		Score
R64	Bye	N/A	W	
R32	Marc-Kevin Goellner (GER)		180	W 6-2, 6-2
R16	Michael Russell (USA)		88	W 6-1, 6-1

Q	Francisco Clavet (ESP)	60	W 4-6, 6-4, 6-2
S	James Blake (USA)	109	W 6-4, 6-0
W	Michel Kratochvil (SUI)	57	W 6-4, 6-2

This Event Points: 250, ATP Ranking: 3, Prize Money: $115,000

SWE v AUS SF, Sydney, Australia; 21.09.2001; DC; Outdoor: Hard; Draw: 6

Round	Opponent	Ranking	Score
RR	Jonas Bjorkman (SWE)	48	W 4-6, 6-4, 7-6, 7-6
RR	Thomas Johansson (SWE)	17	W 7-6(3), 5-7, 6-2, 6-1

This Event Points: , ATP Ranking: 3, Prize Money: $

US Open, NY, U.S.A.; 27.08.2001; GS; Outdoor: Hard; Draw: 128

Round	Opponent	Ranking	Score
R128	Magnus Gustafsson (SWE)	81	W 6-3, 6-2, 7-5
R64	James Blake (USA)	95	W 6-4, 3-6, 2-6, 6-3, 6-0
R32	Albert Portas (ESP)	25	W 6-1, 6-3, 6-4
R16	Tommy Haas (GER)	15	W 3-6, 7-6(2), 6-4, 6-2

Q	Andy Roddick (USA)	18	W 6-7(5), 6-3, 6-4, 3-6, 6-4
S	Yevgeny Kafelnikov (RUS)	7	W 6-1, 6-2, 6-1
W	Pete Sampras (USA)	10	W 7-6(4), 6-1, 6-1

This Event Points: 1,000, ATP Ranking: 4, Prize Money: $850,000

Indianapolis, IN, U.S.A.; 13.08.2001; CS; Outdoor: Hard; Draw: 56

Round	Opponent	Ranking	Score
R64	Bye N/A	W	
R32	Taylor Dent (USA)	127	W 6-2, 7-6(3)
R16	Younes El Aynaoui (MAR)	49	L 3-6, 7-6(1), 3-6

This Event Points: 25, ATP Ranking: 4, Prize Money: $8,830

ATP Masters Series Cincinnati, Ohio, USA; 06.08.2001; SU; Outdoor: Hard; Draw: 64

Round	Opponent	Ranking	Score
R64	Magnus Norman (SWE)	23	W 6-4, 6-1
R32	Bohdan Ulihrach (CZE)	37	W 6-2, 5-7, 6-2
R16	Max Mirnyi (BLR)	47	W 1-6, 6-4, 7-6(5)

Q	Ivan Ljubicic (CRO)	67	W 7-6(3), 6-7(3), 6-4
S	Patrick Rafter (AUS)	7	L 4-6, 3-6

This Event Points: 225, ATP Ranking: 5, Prize Money: $111,200

ATP Masters Series Canada, Montreal, Canada; 30.07.2001; SU; Outdoor: Hard; Draw: 64

Round	Opponent	Ranking	Score
R64	Simon Larose (CAN)	306	W 6-0, 5-7, 6-3
R32	Hicham Arazi (MAR)	34	L 1-6, 4-6

This Event Points: 35, ATP Ranking: 5, Prize Money: $16,250

Wimbledon, England; 25.06.2001; GS; Outdoor: Grass; Draw: 128

Round	Opponent	Ranking	Score
R128	Magnus Gustafsson (SWE)	57	W 6-1, 6-2, 6-4
R64	Taylor Dent (USA)	143	W 1-6, 7-5, 6-3, 6-7(2), 6-3
R32	Younes El Aynaoui (MAR)	82	W 7-5, 5-7, 6-4, 7-6(4)
R16	Nicolas Escude (FRA)	38	L 6-4, 4-6, 3-6, 6-4, 4-6

This Event Points: 150, ATP Ranking: 5, Prize Money: $49,434

's-Hertogenbosch, The Netherlands; 18.06.2001; WS;
Outdoor: Grass; Draw: 32

Round	Opponent	Ranking	Score
R32	Davide Sanguinetti (ITA)	67	W 6-2, 6-1
R16	Goran Ivanisevic (CRO)	128	W 6-4, 7-5
Q	Gilles Elseneer (BEL)	323	W 6-2, 6-4
S	Roger Federer (SUI)	15	W 6-4, 6-2
W	Guillermo Canas (ARG)	61	W 6-3, 6-4

This Event Points: 175, ATP Ranking: 6, Prize Money:
$54,000

London / Queen's Club, England; 11.06.2001; WS; Outdoor:
Grass; Draw: 56

Round	Opponent	Ranking	Score
R64	Bye	N/A	W
R32	Xavier Malisse (BEL)	56	W 6-4, 6-3
R16	Byron Black (ZIM)	64	W 6-3, 6-2
Q	Greg Rusedski (GBR)	46	W 6-4, 6-4
S	Pete Sampras (USA)	4	W 3-6, 6-3, 6-2
W	Tim Henman (GBR)	11	W 7-6(3), 7-6(3)

This Event Points: 225, ATP Ranking: 6, Prize Money:
$91,500

Roland Garros, France; 28.05.2001; GS; Outdoor: Clay; Draw: 128

Round	Opponent	Ranking	Score
R128	Paul-Henri Mathieu (FRA)	238	W 7-6(2), 4-6, 6-3, 6-2
R64	Nikolay Davydenko (RUS)	116	W 6-0, 6-1, 6-3
R32	Andy Roddick (USA)	48	W 6-7(6), 6-4, 2-2 RET
R16	Guillermo Canas (ARG)	82	W 3-6, 6-7(3), 6-2, 6-3, 6-3
Q	Juan Carlos Ferrero (ESP)	4	L 4-6, 2-6, 1-6

This Event Points: 250, ATP Ranking: 6, Prize Money: $78,618

World Team Cup, Dusseldorf, Germany; 21.05.2001; WT; Outdoor: Clay; Draw: 64

Round	Opponent	Ranking	Score
RR	Alex Corretja (ESP)	13	L 6-3, 2-6, 3-6
RR	Magnus Norman (SWE)	9	W 6-1, 6-2
RR	Tommy Haas (GER)	23	L 6-7(5), 6-3, 3-6
W	Marat Safin (RUS)	2	W 6-3, 6-4

This Event Points: , ATP Ranking: 6, Prize Money: $195,000

ATP Masters Series Hamburg, Germany; 14.05.2001; SU;
Outdoor: Clay; Draw: 64

Round	Opponent	Ranking	Score
R64	Arnaud Di Pasquale (FRA)	64	W 6-3, 6-2
R32	Fernando Vicente (ESP)	46	W 3-6, 6-2, 6-4
R16	Andrew Ilie (AUS)	58	W 6-2, 7-6(2)
Q	Franco Squillari (ARG)	19	W 6-4, 6-2
S	Albert Portas (ESP)	42	L 6-3, 5-7, 2-6

This Event Points: 225, ATP Ranking: 7, Prize Money:
$111,200

ATP Masters Series Rome, Italy; 07.05.2001; SU; Outdoor:
Clay; Draw: 64

Round	Opponent	Ranking	Score
R64	Bohdan Ulihrach (CZE)	40	W 6-1, 2-6, 7-5
R32	Tommy Haas (GER)	22	W 7-5, 6-3
R16	Alex Corretja (ESP)	11	L 6-7(2), 4-6

This Event Points: 75, ATP Ranking: 7, Prize Money: $30,800

AUS v BRA WG QF, Florianapolis; 06.04.2001; DC; Outdoor:
Clay; Draw: 4

Round	Opponent	Ranking	Score
RR	Fernando Meligeni (BRA)	95	W 6-3, 6-3, 6-3
RR	Gustavo Kuerten (BRA)	2	W 7-6(5), 6-3, 7-6(3)

This Event Points: , ATP Ranking: 7, Prize Money: $

ATP Masters Series Miami, FL, U.S.A.; 19.03.2001; SU; Outdoor: Hard; Draw: 96

Round	Opponent	Ranking	Score
R128	Bye N/A	W	
R64	Jacobo Diaz (ESP)	121	W 6-3, 6-3
R32	Nicolas Lapentti (ECU)	28	W 6-3, 6-3
R16	Fabrice Santoro (FRA)	52	W 3-6, 6-1, 6-2
Q	Andy Roddick (USA)	119	W 6-3, 6-2
S	Jan-Michael Gambill (USA)	19	L 5-7, 4-6

This Event Points: 225, ATP Ranking: 7, Prize Money: $123,000

ATP Masters Series Indian Wells, California, USA; 12.03.2001; SU; Outdoor: Hard; Draw: 64

Round	Opponent	Ranking	Score
R64	Albert Costa (ESP)	34	W 6-2, 5-7, 6-1

R32	Paradorn Srichaphan (THA)	121	W 6-3, 6-3
R16	Bohdan Ulihrach (CZE)	54	W 6-2, 6-4
Q	Nicolas Escude (FRA)	36	W 6-1, 6-3
S	Andre Agassi (USA) 4		L 4-6, 6-3, 4-6

This Event Points: 225, ATP Ranking: 8, Prize Money: $111,200

Scottsdale, AZ, U.S.A.; 05.03.2001; WS; Outdoor: Hard; Draw: 32

Round	Opponent	Ranking	Score
R32	David Sanchez (ESP)	86	W 6-1, 6-3
R16	Richard Fromberg (AUS)	125	W 3-6, 6-1, 6-3
Q	Marcelo Rios (CHI)	25	W 7-5, 6-2
S	Francisco Clavet (ESP)	40	L 3-6, 4-6

This Event Points: 75, ATP Ranking: 6, Prize Money: $18,400

San Jose, CA, U.S.A.; 26.02.2001; WS; Indoor: Hard; Draw: 32

Round	Opponent	Ranking	Score
R32	Sebastien Lareau (CAN)	94	W 6-3, 6-1
R16	Andrei Stoliarov (RUS)	95	W 6-2, 6-7(8),

6-3

Q   Greg Rusedski (GBR) 58   L 7-5, 1-6, 4-6

This Event Points: 40, ATP Ranking: 6, Prize Money: $10,800

AUS v ECU WG Rd 1, Perth, Australia; 09.02.2001; DC;
Outdoor: Grass; Draw: 4

Round	Opponent	Ranking	Score
RR	Giovanni Lapentti (ECU)	927	W 6-3, 6-2, 6-2
RR	Nicolas Lapentti (ECU)	25	W 6-2, 6-1, 6-1

This Event Points: , ATP Ranking: 6, Prize Money: $

Australian Open, Australia; 15.01.2001; GS; Outdoor: Hard;
Draw: 128

Round	Opponent	Ranking	Score
R128	Jonas Bjorkman (SWE)	41	W 7-5, 4-6, 2-6, 6-3, 6-2
R64	Tommy Haas (GER)	20	W 7-5, 7-6(5), 6-4
R32	Carlos Moya (ESP)	42	L 6-4, 1-6, 7-5, 2-6, 5-7

This Event Points: 75, ATP Ranking: 7, Prize Money: $18,086

Sydney, Australia; 08.01.2001; WS; Outdoor: Hard; Draw: 32

Round	Opponent	Ranking	Score

R32	Wayne Arthurs (AUS)	84	W 6-7(3), 7-6(5), 6-2
R16	Andrew Ilie (AUS)	48	W 6-4, 6-1
Q	Fabrice Santoro (FRA)	46	W 6-4, 6-1
S	Sebastien Grosjean (FRA)	19	W 6-3, 4-6, 6-4
W	Magnus Norman (SWE)	4	W 6-4, 6-1

This Event Points: 175, ATP Ranking: 7, Prize Money: $54,000

Adelaide, Australia; 01.01.2001; WS; Outdoor: Hard; Draw: 32

Round	Opponent	Ranking	Score
R32	Wayne Arthurs (AUS)	83	W 6-4, 6-3
R16	Bjorn Phau (GER)	208	W 6-7(5), 6-4, 6-0
Q	Tommy Haas (GER)	23	L 4-6, 6-0, 1-6

This Event Points: 40, ATP Ranking: 7, Prize Money: $10,100

Lleyton Hewitt's Match Record for 2002

Tennis Masters Cup, Shanghai, China; 11.11.2002; WC; Indoor: Hard; Draw: 8

Round	Opponent	Ranking	Score
RR	Albert Costa (ESP)	11	W 6-2, 4-6, 6-3
RR	Carlos Moya (ESP)	5	L 4-6, 5-7
RR	Marat Safin (RUS)	3	W 6-4, 2-6, 6-4
S	Roger Federer (SUI)	6	W 7-5, 5-7, 7-5
W	Juan Carlos Ferrero (ESP)	4	W 7-5, 7-5, 2-6, 2-6, 6-4

This Event Points: 650, ATP Ranking: 1, Prize Money: $1,400,000

ATP Masters Series Paris, France; 28.10.2002; SU; Indoor: Carpet; Draw: 48

Round	Opponent	Ranking	Score
R64	Bye	N/A	W
R32	Jarkko Nieminen (FIN)	42	W 6-2, 6-4
R16	Yevgeny Kafelnikov (RUS)	15	W 6-2, 7-6(3)
Q	Roger Federer (SUI)	8	W 6-4, 6-4
S	Paradorn Srichaphan (THA)	21	W 6-3, 3-6, 6-3

F   Marat Safin (RUS)   5   L 6-7(4), 0-6, 4-6

This Event Points: 350, ATP Ranking: 1, Prize Money: $211,000

Stockholm, Sweden; 21.10.2002; WS; Indoor: Hard; Draw: 32

Round	Opponent	Ranking	Score
R32	Thomas Enqvist (SWE)	37	W W/O
R16	Raemon Sluiter (NED)	76	L 3-6, 3-6

This Event Points: 15, ATP Ranking: 1, Prize Money: $10,200

Tokyo, Japan; 30.09.2002; CS; Outdoor: Hard; Draw: 56

Round	Opponent	Ranking	Score
R64	Bye N/A	W	
R32	Michael Chang (USA)	126	W 6-2, 6-2
R16	Nicolas Massu (CHI)	60	W 6-7(4), 6-2, 6-4
Q	Paradorn Srichaphan (THA)	31	L 4-6, 3-6

This Event Points: 60, ATP Ranking: 1, Prize Money: $16,280

AUS v. IND WG Q, Adelaide, Australia; 20.09.2002; DC; Outdoor: Hard; Draw: 6

Round	Opponent	Ranking	Score
RR	Harsh Mankad (IND)	831	W 6-1, 7-6(2), 6-1

This Event Points: , ATP Ranking: 1, Prize Money: $

US Open, NY, U.S.A.; 26.08.2002; GS; Outdoor: Hard; Draw: 128

Round	Opponent	Ranking	Score
R128	Nicolas Coutelot (FRA)	101	W 6-2, 6-3, 6-3
R64	Noam Okun (ISR)	114	W 7-6(7), 6-4, 6-1
R32	James Blake (USA)	26	W 6-7(5), 6-3, 6-4, 3-6, 6-3
R16	Jiri Novak (CZE)	14	W 6-4, 6-2, 7-5
Q	Younes El Aynaoui (MAR)	20	W 6-1, 7-6(6), 4-6, 6-2
S	Andre Agassi (USA)	6	L 4-6, 6-7(5), 7-6(1), 2-6

This Event Points: 450, ATP Ranking: 1, Prize Money: $250,000

Indianapolis, IN, U.S.A.; 12.08.2002; CS; Outdoor: Hard; Draw: 56

Round	Opponent	Ranking	Score
R64	Bye	N/A	W
R32	Alberto Martin (ESP)	68	W 6-3, 7-5
R16	Greg Rusedski (GBR)	41	L 6-7(3), 4-6

This Event Points: 25, ATP Ranking: 1, Prize Money: $8,550

ATP Masters Series Cincinnati, Ohio, USA; 05.08.2002; SU; Outdoor: Hard; Draw: 64

Round	Opponent	Ranking	Score
R64	Robby Ginepri (USA)	108	W 6-0, 6-0
R32	Davide Sanguinetti (ITA)	53	W 5-0 RET
R16	Jarkko Nieminen (FIN)	35	W 2-6, 6-2, 6-3
Q	Andre Agassi (USA)	6	W 7-5, 6-3
S	Fernando Gonzalez (CHI)	39	W 6-7(3), 7-5, 6-2
F	Carlos Moya (ESP)	17	L 5-7, 6-7(5)

This Event Points: 350, ATP Ranking: 1, Prize Money: $206,000

ATP Masters Series Canada, Toronto, Canada; 29.07.2002; SU; Outdoor: Hard; Draw: 64

Round	Opponent	Ranking	Score
R64	Felix Mantilla (ESP)	55	L 6-2, 4-6, 3-6

This Event Points: 5, ATP Ranking: 1, Prize Money: $8,325

Wimbledon, England; 24.06.2002; GS; Outdoor: Grass; Draw: 128

Round	Opponent	Ranking	Score

Round	Opponent	Ranking	Score
R128	Jonas Bjorkman (SWE)	47	W 6-4, 7-5, 6-1
R64	Gregory Carraz (FRA)	168	W 6-4, 7-6(5), 6-2
R32	Julian Knowle (AUT)	95	W 6-2, 6-1, 6-3
R16	Mikhail Youzhny (RUS)	61	W 6-3, 6-3, 7-5
Q	Sjeng Schalken (NED)	23	W 6-2, 6-2, 6-7(5), 1-6, 7-5
S	Tim Henman (GBR)	5	W 7-5, 6-1, 7-5
W	David Nalbandian (ARG)	32	W 6-1, 6-3, 6-2

This Event Points: 1,000, ATP Ranking: 1, Prize Money: $786,140

's-Hertogenbosch, The Netherlands; 17.06.2002; WS; Outdoor: Grass; Draw: 32

Round	Opponent	Ranking	Score
R32	Michael Chang (USA)	97	W 7-6(2), 7-6(4)
R16	Mikhail Youzhny (RUS)	61	W 6-4, 5-7, 7-6(4)
Q	Arnaud Clement (FRA)	42	L W/O

This Event Points: 40, ATP Ranking: 1, Prize Money: $9,940

London / Queen's Club, England; 10.06.2002; WS; Outdoor: Grass; Draw: 56

Round	Opponent	Ranking	Score

Round	Opponent	Ranking	Score
R64	Bye N/A		W
R32	Mardy Fish (USA)	148	W 7-5, 6-3
R16	Olivier Rochus (BEL)	65	W 6-2, 6-1
Q	Todd Martin (USA)	44	W 7-6(4), 7-5
S	Sjeng Schalken (NED)	34	W 7-6(5), 6-3
W	Tim Henman (GBR)	5	W 4-6, 6-1, 6-4

This Event Points: 225, ATP Ranking: 1, Prize Money: $84,200

Roland Garros, France; 27.05.2002; GS; Outdoor: Clay; Draw: 128

Round	Opponent	Ranking	Score
R128	Andre Sa (BRA)	83	W 7-5, 6-4, 7-5
R64	Andrei Stoliarov (RUS)	109	W 4-6, 7-6(5), 6-0, 7-5
R32	Sjeng Schalken (NED)	33	W 6-1, 7-5, 6-7(3), 6-1
R16	Guillermo Canas (ARG)	17	L 7-6(1), 6-7(13), 4-6, 3-6

This Event Points: 150, ATP Ranking: 1, Prize Money: $50,624

ATP Masters Series Hamburg, Germany; 13.05.2002; SU; Outdoor: Clay; Draw: 64

Round	Opponent	Ranking	Score

Round	Opponent	Ranking	Score
R64	Philipp Kohlschreiber (GER)	426	W 7-5, 6-4
R32	Bjorn Phau (GER)	138	W 6-3, 6-3
R16	Jiri Novak (CZE)	15	W 6-4, 6-3
Q	Marat Safin (RUS)	5	L 3-6, 1-6

This Event Points: 125, ATP Ranking: 1, Prize Money: $54,280

ATP Masters Series Rome, Italy; 06.05.2002; SU; Outdoor: Clay; Draw: 64

Round	Opponent	Ranking	Score
R64	Jonas Bjorkman (SWE)	59	W 6-2, 6-3
R32	Carlos Moya (ESP)	25	L 3-6, 2-6

This Event Points: 35, ATP Ranking: 1, Prize Money: $15,000

Barcelona, Spain; 22.04.2002; CS; Outdoor: Clay; Draw: 56

Round	Opponent	Ranking	Score
R64	Bye	N/A	W
R32	Marc Lopez (ESP)	131	W 7-6(6), 6-2
R16	David Nalbandian (ARG)	31	W 6-2, 6-4
Q	Younes El Aynaoui (MAR)	19	W 6-4, 6-2
S	Gaston Gaudio (ARG)	64	L 4-6, 5-7

This Event Points: 135, ATP Ranking: 1, Prize Money: $37,750

ATP Masters Series Monte Carlo, Monaco; 15.04.2002; SU; Outdoor: Clay; Draw: 64

Round	Opponent	Ranking	Score
R64	Carlos Moya (ESP)	26	L 4-6, 3-6

This Event Points: 5, ATP Ranking: 1, Prize Money: $7,900

ATP Masters Series Miami, FL, U.S.A.; 18.03.2002; SU; Outdoor: Hard; Draw: 96

Round	Opponent	Ranking	Score
R128	Bye	N/A	W
R64	Paradorn Srichaphan (THA)	67	W 7-6(3), 7-5
R32	Jan-Michael Gambill (USA)	29	W 3-6, 6-4, 7-5
R16	James Blake (USA)	49	W 6-4, 6-1
Q	Marat Safin (RUS)	7	W 2-6, 6-2, 7-6(4)
S	Roger Federer (SUI)	14	L 3-6, 4-6

This Event Points: 225, ATP Ranking: 1, Prize Money: $126,050

ATP Masters Series Indian Wells, California, USA; 11.03.2002; SU; Outdoor: Hard; Draw: 64

Round	Opponent	Ranking	Score
R64	Carlos Moya (ESP)	24	W 6-4, 6-4
R32	Andrei Pavel (ROU)	31	W 4-6, 6-3, 6-0
R16	Jan-Michael Gambill (USA)	27	W 6-2, 6-4
Q	Thomas Enqvist (SWE)	22	W 6-4, 6-4
S	Pete Sampras (USA)	13	W 6-2, 6-4
W	Tim Henman (GBR)	11	W 6-1, 6-2

This Event Points: 500, ATP Ranking: 1, Prize Money: $392,000

San Jose, CA, U.S.A.; 25.02.2002; WS; Indoor: Hard; Draw: 32

Round	Opponent	Ranking	Score
R32	Michael Llodra (FRA)	116	W 6-2, 3-6, 6-2
R16	Paradorn Srichaphan (THA)	73	W 6-7(2), 6-4, 7-6(6)
Q	Todd Martin (USA)	70	W 6-3, 7-5
S	Jan-Michael Gambill (USA)	22	W 7-5, 6-4
W	Andre Agassi (USA)	5	W 4-6, 7-6(6), 7-6(4)

This Event Points: 175, ATP Ranking: 1, Prize Money: $51,500

Australian Open, Australia; 14.01.2002; GS; Outdoor: Hard; Draw: 128

Round	Opponent	Ranking	Score
R128	Alberto Martin (ESP)	39	L 6-1, 1-6, 4-6, 6-7(4)

This Event Points: 5, ATP Ranking: 1, Prize Money: $7,790

SOURCE: www.ATPWORLDTOUR.com

Chapter 6: The Jason Stoltenberg Perspective

Lleyton Hewitt's former coach Jason Stoltenberg attended the 2013 U.S. Open as a coach for a young Australian player. Stoltenberg took time out to discuss his memories of the career of Hewitt for this book.

Question: Your first memory of Lleyton Hewitt?

Jason Stoltenberg: "I actually played Lleyton in the final when he won Adelaide. So I played him when he was sixteen. That was my first experience with him. And I was extremely impressed, obviously. My first real memory I suppose is watching him go toe-to-toe with Agassi in the semis of the same tournament. And Andre was coming back, he wasn't at his best but Agassi's Agassi. And Lleyton beat him 6 and 6. And I remember thinking, Well for him to even think that he has a chance...I mean he should be over-awed just being on the same court as Agassi."

"The thing that struck me is that he played the ball, not the player. I think that's a pretty special quality. He actually still somehow thought he had a chance to win. At sixteen...against the guy who's this multiple slam winner, like a legend of the game. And I played him and lost 7-6 in the third. And just extremely tenacious, just a very special kid."

Question: You played him other times?

Jason Stoltenberg: "I played him four times. I played him in Newport and beat him on grass when he was a little kid...I also bring that up to him quite a bit [smiles]. And then he beat me in the final of Sydney, we played in another final around '99. I think he beat me again in Adelaide, maybe the semifinal. But I found him very difficult to play. And to be honest, when I finished my own career, one of the reasons - not the main reason - but one of the reasons why I retired was because I felt like there were certain players that I couldn't beat. And he was one of them. And I never felt that before. I was getting older. When he was in his prime he was a difficult guy to beat. Just a great counterpuncher, gave you nothing. And he was never out. You never had him. It didn't matter how big a serve, how big a game you got, what the score is, you never had him. And I think he was probably, if not **the best**, clearly one of the best one-on-one competitors I've ever seen. In my time. Very, very special in that case."

Question: How do you think he became like that?

Jason Stoltenberg: "I don't know. I think his family is obviously very competitive. His parents played sport. And I think a lot of that stuff is in him. He grew up with a sort of football background and just loved the competition. Still does. Doesn't go away."

Question: Do you have an on or off court memory that captures his essence?

Jason Stoltenberg: "Well, I coached him when he was No. 1 for about eighteen months. And to sit courtside and watch him play as much as I did was a real treat. I saw him come back from situations where nobody would have even seen a glimmer of light. You thought he was done. And he just somehow...he has a real good ability to stay in the moment and not get too far ahead of himself. That's a special quality I think a lot of the really great players have. I was there when he won Wimbledon. That was a very special moment. To be there with him for that."

"But there was one tournament that stuck out for me - the Masters Cup in Shanghai 2002. He had a tough group - Safin, Carlos Costa and Moya. And Moya and Safin were big guys that troubled him with their power. And he beat Costa, lost to Moya. And I think he had to beat Safin to make the semis. And he beat Safin in three. And then he beat Roger in the semis. And then Ferrero in the final in five. And that kind of wrapped Lleyton up to me. Because he was on empty. He had nothing left. He played a long year. He was desperate to finish No. 1. And he had to secure it at that tournament. And Wimbledon was special, because it was Wimbledon, just the amount of effort that went into winning that, the matches he came back from, considering the best eight players in the world. That was the best week for me. That was amazing. Didn't surprise me. But to see him do it. That was Lleyton in a nutshell."

Question: Is there a certain match in particular, that stands out, where Hewitt was down and out but came back?

Jason Stoltenberg: "Oh, there's a million of them. The Davis Cup match when he beat Federer in Melbourne. (Two sets down, two points away from defeat.) Yeah. That was one. That probably really stood out in his mind, I think. Because Roger was really up and about then. That was 2003. Roger was just becoming Roger. And he wouldn't have lost too many at that point...Lleyton in his backyard, in his element, playing in Australia in front of the fanatics. Against the best player in the world. And he still sees the light. Somehow he still sees the light that no one else would see. Somehow he just hangs, he stays patient. Anyone else seems to be gone, he's out there competing and he's calm, he just doesn't panic. And I think that meant a lot to Roger too, in his career, too. I don't think Roger lost to him in fifteen times after that. I think he might have made a point to himself: Okay, I'm not going to lose to this little bugger ever again. That was one match that stood out. I was commentating that match."

Question: You know Lleyton. Is there anything that surprises you about him?

Jason Stoltenberg: "Well, I know him obviously since before I started coaching him. Because I played him and been around him a lot. And he's actually quite a quiet sort of guy. A mellow guy. You'd think he was this 'Bouncing off the walls' sort of guy but he's actually not. He's a pretty nice guy. And he's not a guy who goes out...there's no skeletons in Lleyton's closet, as they say. He's very straight down the line. He's always been very professional. Never goes out, never gets into trouble. He's really quite a respectful young man. That's what I found. And I think that's a side of him that people don't see. Or haven't seen. They just see the guy on the court."

"At times he's had the white line fever - he walks over that white line and he turns into this competitive animal. And off the court he can be quiet. And very private. So that's probably something people would be surprised about. But he's earned everything he's got, there's no question about that. He's a champion. Seventy-something weeks at No. 1. Finished No. 1 couple years in a row. Won the Masters Cup twice. Won two slams. The guy is 5-foot-10, he's giving up a lot of power. I think he did amazingly well. I think he's had a great career. I think he'll be remembered as a great player. A lot of people will remember him because he was unique. He's just such a fighter. There's a lot of fighters around but he was just a bit different."

Hewitt leads series 4-1

1998   Adelaide   F Hewitt 36 63 76

1998   Newport   R16 Stoltenberg   61 63

1999   Adelaide   SF   Hewitt   61 63

2000   Adelaide   QF   Hewitt   62 62

2000   Sydney   F   Hewitt 64 60

Chapter 7: Memorable Hewitt quotes

"I was 700 in the world. Just luckily, I was playing a Perth challenger one week. Next thing I knew, I was playing Agassi in the semifinal. And, really, I suppose it all happened too quick for me to realize that I've jumped 600 spots. But I suppose the biggest part is being the second year, I haven't really fallen down yet. I had a great start for the year and hopefully it continues in the second half of the year."

***

Q. Lleyton, this is your first year (1999) in Davis Cup. How different is the feeling being in the final and can you tell about how excited, how motivated you are?

LLEYTON HEWITT: "Well, it's an unbelievable feeling for me. A lot of the players go through their careers without playing in a Davis Cup final. For me, at the age of 18 to have this opportunity, in my third tie, when at the start of the year it looked like I was going to be struggling for a spot, you know, this is definitely the biggest moment in my career so far."

***

"For me, I come from a football background. It's the only time, you know, being a tennis player that you get to come together as a team. You know, that means a lot to me. I played team sports growing up. I just like, you know, being in the changing rooms, getting all the boys pumped up before the matches. You have your bad days and have you your good days, but that's been the big thing for us this year. We've all stepped up at different times. That's the biggest enjoyment I have of playing the Davis Cup. It is sort of a team atmosphere and it's that team feeling in the changing rooms."

***

"I was very nervous, I suppose, in the changing rooms. I wasn't able to be out there and enjoy as it as I would have liked to be. But to see Mark play that well today under that kind of pressure, you know, in a Davis Cup final, it's a fantastic honor, I think, for me to be alongside Philippoussis and the Woodies here, winning my first Davis Cup trophy at the age of 18, in my third Davis Cup tie."

***

"We're all different people. But (Roger)'s a great bloke. I get along really well with Roger. He's very down to Earth. I think that's probably the best quality he has. He's very easy to get along with. I always say G'day to him, have a chat. He's a really nice guy."

***

"Museums? I'm not really into museums right at the moment (smiling). Yeah, I don't know. I'm going back to Australia and I'll put the feet up for a bit and then start training pretty hard."

***

"I'm obviously very competitive and love getting out there and, you know, trying to improve my game as well. I think Roger has obviously tried to take the game to another level. You've got to keep working and work on your weaknesses and try and improve those to stay with the best guys and stay at the top of the game."

***

Q. Could you compare how you're playing at this stage to the way you were playing in 2001...

LLEYTON HEWITT: "Well, I'll answer it for the fifteenth time this week. There's times when I'm playing as well as then. Yeah, at the moment, I'm playing pretty solid tennis day in, day out. You know, back then, you know, in the semis or final when I played here, I played pretty faultless tennis both those matches. If I can keep doing that in the next three matches, then I'll be close."

***

Q. You say a lot of times you've been working on your serve hard with your coach. What exactly have you been doing?

LLEYTON HEWITT: "Just, you know, ball toss, you know getting in the mind frame of using my legs a bit more out there, pushing up through the serve. Just, you know, small reminders more than anything. But, you know, just trying to focus on that and get in a routine, I guess, so when you go out there in the match it's second nature."

***

Q. Aside from the tennis, what do you like about being here in New York? How have you been spending your

time off court?

LLEYTON HEWITT: "Stuck in traffic (smiling). No, you know, it's great. It's a big city. It's a great place to visit. But I really haven't done a lot of sight-seeing that much. Last week I was going out to Long Island every day to play out there. And, you know, this week I've just been -- you come here on your off-day anyway. By the time you get out here, practice, stretch, watch a match or two, have some lunch, it's time to go back, have a massage, and get ready to play the next day. Yeah, so I've done very little sight-seeing."

***

Q. Wayne Arthurs strikes me as one of the good guys in your sport. He's tried to give something back to the younger players. How sad is it to see him retiring?

LLEYTON HEWITT: "Yeah, you know, it's disappointing. Wayne's had an awesome career. I get along really well with Wayne off the court, as well. He's a guy that I've practiced with a lot in the past. You know, he really -- I think he gets along extremely well with everyone, on and off the court. There's always going to come a time, though, when your body's just not quite the same and you've got to step away from the sport. He's the only person who knows when that time's right. But, you know, he's been a great ambassador for the sport of tennis for a number of years now."

***

Q. Is Adam Scott a mate of yours? What do you think of him going into the final round of the TPC with a chance to win that?

LLEYTON HEWITT: "Yeah, I met Adam at the Australian

PGA in December (2003). He's a great kid. He's a very likable kid. Yeah, he is a helluva player. I've been watching a little bit, and I've got no doubt - I don't know what it is now - but if he plays the way he did yesterday, then he's going to be in pretty good stead. It's going to take a pretty good player to beat him."

**

Q. As a guy for whom consistency and consistent approach is obviously a virtue of your game, do you have a hard time identifying with a player like Safin, whose motivation seems to come in and out, up and down? Do you say, "How can someone possibly not care all the time"?

LLEYTON HEWITT: "Not really. Everyone's personality is different, I guess. That's what makes the game so interesting I guess in a lot of ways. Yeah, you're always going to have those kind of characters out there, I guess. You know, different personalities. You know, you look at McEnroe and Borg, totally different situations, playing styles, strengths and weaknesses, I guess. Obviously, Marat, one of his biggest strengths is how hard he can hit the ball, his power, his all court game. Sometimes the mental side of it lets him down sometimes. If you got the whole package, then you'd be winning week in and week out, I guess. It would be boring for everyone."

**

Q. In what way are the balls causing more problem? Is it the fact they are getting so heavy?

LLEYTON HEWITT: "They're massive. They're ridiculous. After like one game against a guy like that, you know -- I've never played with balls that are getting that big. It's as simple as that. I thought the balls in Rotterdam were quite heavy till I came here. You know, the court's definitely, you know, it's a little bit rough out there. That's always going to chop the balls up a little bit more than a smoother court, such as a US Open hard court. But, you know, there's no reason why the ball should get, you know, that heavy. I know a lot of players complained early on when I got here first couple of days that were hitting them. You know, it was a joke. They complained. They said they got other boxes. I haven't noticed a huge change."

***

Q. When Goran played that final against Patrick Rafter, did you watch it? Where were you? What were you feeling?

LLEYTON HEWITT: "Yeah, I was somewhere in another country, you know, watching on TV. You know, obviously it was weird because I felt Pat was probably the better player for most of the match. He was the one, you know, fought steady, got on top of Goran. You know, I felt like he -- I just felt that he was going to have, you know, more opportunities to break Goran than Goran was having to break Pat. As it turned out, yeah, Goran played a great game to break, and then Pat had chances to break back. It's a tough match to watch, I guess."

Q. Did you have some emotion for Patrick?

LLEYTON HEWITT: "Oh, for sure. You know, I've known Pat, yeah, so long and looked up to him. You know, and I think I knew how much he wanted to win this title here, you know, and lost in the final the year before to Pete. Yeah, it was awkward watching the whole match."

***

Q. Do you like it when there's a big crowd making a lot of noise, most of it for your opponent?

LLEYTON HEWITT: "Oh, doesn't worry me, mate."

***

Q. How would you like to see the match against Goran go in terms of strategy?

LLEYTON HEWITT: "I'd just like to win."

Q. Is there anything you'd like to see happen?

LLEYTON HEWITT: "You won't find out."

***

Hewitt quotes after beating 20-year-old Donald Young 7-5 6-2 in the first round in Washington DC in 2009:

"He's very talented and he just hasn't fulfilled his potential just yet. It's a big step up from juniors to seniors. He's lightning quick, gets to a lot of balls, and is starting to get a bigger game out there. He's just not playing the big points very well just yet."

***

Hewitt on Vince Spadea's remarkable comeback:
"You've got to take your hat off to Vince (Spadea). Hell of an effort for what he's done. The way he's come back after losing so many first rounds there for a while (Spadea lost an ATP-record 21 consecutive matches from October 1999 through June 2000). He obviously broke the drought there

against Greg Rusedski at Wimbledon a couple of years back, but we didn't see him for a while after that. He was playing the Challengers and the Futures.   The way he's bounced back and gone about his business very quietly, sort of got his ranking back up there, it's pretty amazing."

***

Hewitt talking about Rafael Nadal before their first match at 2004 Australian Open.

Q. Nadal, your next opponent, what do you know about him?

LLEYTON HEWITT: Very talented young player. Yeah, what I've heard, what I've seen - little bits I've seen - he's a hell of a prospect coming up. It's going to be a tough match. I've got to go up to another level, I think. I look forward to the challenge, though.

Q. There's a bit of talk about him. Is there talk amongst the players about him coming up?

LLEYTON HEWITT: Yeah, I think so. Probably more so -- you know, I probably heard a little more from the media, whatever, maybe last year sometime when he had some pretty good wins over Moya and I think Costa maybe on clay, as well. So clay's his number one surface at the moment. But he had a pretty good run at Wimbledon. I watched a couple of his matches there on TV. He played pretty well on grass, for his first time on grass. He seems like he's got a really good head on him, as well. He's handled the expectation and the pressures very well. You know, he's just one of the next Spaniards coming up. There's a lot of them.

***

Hewitt talking about Nadal after the 2004 Australian Open match.

Q. You were saying out there that you expect a tough match. Was it even tougher than you thought, the young boy tonight?

LLEYTON HEWITT: Yeah. I seen a little bit of his second-round match. He played a lot better tonight than he did in that second-round match, I tell you. He could have very easily been down two sets to one in that match against Ascione, I think, the French bloke. And it wasn't until the other guy started getting a few cramps that he actually got on top of him. He really went up another couple of levels tonight. Yeah, he's a great player. As I said before, you know, all the good stuff you've heard and seen in the past, you know, he's going to be very good in a couple of years.

***

Hewitt talking about Nadal before their 2005 Australian Open match.

Q. Your thoughts on your next match, Nadal?

LLEYTON HEWITT: Yeah, doesn't get any easier. Just another step up, I guess. Yeah, he was obviously a little bit fortunate a couple of days ago to get out of that match against Youzhny. But then tonight, from all accounts, you know, he's destroyed a guy that, you know, he probably should destroy, as well. It's going to be a tough match. He's a worthy opponent, playing Round of 16 in a Grand Slam, on any surface, I think. And he's hungry, he really is. You know, he loves going out there, playing big matches. That's something that I really respect in, you know, a young guy like him, you know, the way that he handles the situation. He played Roddick at the US Open in a night match, and I thought he handled himself really well in that situation. Davis Cup final in Spain, that's not an easy thing to do, to play in a final at such a young age. He handled it incredibly well. I don't think the situation is going to worry him too much. Plus, we also had a tough match here last year in the third round so...

Q. What is his potential? Is he going to be up there with you top guys pretty soon?

LLEYTON HEWITT: I think so. He's been -- at least last year, I think the year before, he might have been injured for the French Open or a lot of the clay court season. He's a lot better player than whatever his ranking is, to not be seeded. He's good on all surfaces. As I said, he's hungry, he's intense, he's competitive, he's all of that, and he's good for the game. I'll be very surprised if he didn't win the French Open one day.

I've looked at a lot of Nadal's matches over the last couple years. The big matches don't worry him. He's that kind of kid. He's like me when I was 16, 17, playing Andre Agassi in front of your home crowd. That was awesome for me. Very similar to him. He didn't take a step back against Roddick at the US Open, maybe the second round they played. He took it to him. Obviously, Andy was too good and too powerful at the time. But, yeah, he doesn't step back for anyone.

***

To Andy Roddick during one of their heated battles:
"Have a crack at it, mate."

Chapter 8:   Hewitt Fans Celebrate The Champion

Hewitt was an amazing talent. More than anyone else, as soon as I saw him, I thought he was destined for greatness. The most impressive things about him were his speed on the court, and his amazing never-say-die attitude. One particular match I wish to mention was his semifinal at the 2002 Masters Cup against Federer. Hewitt was cruising as he served for the match at 7-5, 5-4, and had match points, but Federer managed to break back, turned on the style, and it turned into an absolute epic. Hewitt just showed amazing resilience, determined not to let anything stop him from winning, and he got the job done 7-5, 5-7, 7-5. I mention this epic match because it now tends to be overshadowed by their even more epic match in the 2003 Davis Cup semifinals.

***

Lleyton is hands down my favorite player, so fun and exciting to watch. He still can go far in slam draws. My favorite Hewitt match... 10-8 in the fifth over Nalbandian.

***

Queens 2000 vs Sampras. Broke Sampras's serve in each set. Who knew that was nothing compared to the U.S. Open the following year where he absolutely annihilated Sampras' serve. I just remember in those two breadstick sets him running down everything Sampras was throwing. Just eating up the low fast balls. He, in my opinion, suffered the most with the surfaces changing. He would have been monstrous on the old Wimbledon and U.S. Open surfaces.

***

4:33 am Classic. Hewitt's whole 2005 Australian Open campaign was such a memorable tournament.

***

Who can forget the grudge match of Hewitt vs. Coria in 2005 Davis Cup? Hewitt won 7-6, 6-1, 1-6, 6-2. Some hilarious mickey taking by both players in that match, and afterwards in their press conferences. One of Hewitt's quotes was "It was very dumb by them to provoke me. Very rarely have I lost matches when people try and get in my face." Coria said "I'd rather not win a single tournament in my life than be like him. He is infuriating, and I felt like killing him on the court."

***

"He was a firebrand in his youth, always a fighter!

Now he's a consummate professional, always a fighter!"

***

Oh, and another few matches, which Hewitt played against El Aynaoui in early 2003. El Aynaoui beat Hewitt at the 2003 Australian Open, in the Round of 16, by 6-7, 7-6, 7-6, 6-4. It was a match of the highest quality. In the first round of 2003 Indian Wells, Hewitt played El Aynaoui, and he had to win to keep his World No. 1 ranking. Hewitt trailed 4-6, 3-5, and looked down and out. El Aynaoui had match points. Somehow, Hewitt dug deep and came all the way back to win 4-6, 7-5, 6-2, and went on to retain the title.

***

2005 fourth round Australian Open vs. Nadal. One of my favorite matches of all time. Pure slugfest and exciting. Booming groundstrokes and Vamos's and Cmons! I thought Hewitt was done after that third set bread stick. Nope. He won the fourth in a tiebreak and there was some kind of crazy drama in that set that I can't remember. Blew out Nadal in the fifth. Great times.

***

I admire Hewitt's toughness, passion and his will. Let's face it he wasn't ever going to win "The Most Politically Correct

Sportsman of the Year" award but he left everything on the tennis court and if today's younger players had half of this guy's fire they'd be right up there with the best currently.

***

I personally feel Hewitt's mental toughness was and still is underrated. Sure, people list him as one of the greats but I think that there isn't anyone with the same degree of toughness as him, not even Nadal. I absolutely despised young Hewitt but I always admired his mental stubbornness to just never give up. It's always something I wished my beloved Safin or Tsonga would have, not to mention if Tomic had the personality that Hewitt did Australia wouldn't be ridiculed like it is with our current crop of youngsters. -Big Red

***

Hewitt became the first baseliner to dominate volleyers in his time. Just look at his stats: Hewitt 5-4 over Sampras (2-1 on grass). Hewitt 3-0 vs. Rafter. Hewitt 3-0 vs. Ivanisevic (3-0 on grass). Hewitt 9-1 vs. Henman (4-0 on grass). Hewitt 1-0 vs. Krajicek. He doesn't get enough credit for what he's done in tennis.   -Martin J.

***

The   first time I saw Lleyton Hewitt play was coaching courtside at the Little Masters in Queensland, he may have been 12 or 13. There was one player from Queensland who was 6-ft 3-inch at 15! (The event was under 16). Basically it was the best State juniors playing each other head to head. My player had several arguments about linecalls with him and to cut a long story short it nearly came to blows. All I remember as I headed them both off at the net were his eyes were black! And the other (Lleyton's) coach saying: "He is always like that." The story really only illustrates his intensity, even then. He won that match but he and my player finished at the end of the field - they were physically much smaller and younger. The first three players in the event were never heard from again. Three years later Lleyton won the S.A. Open at 15, qualifying later at the Oz Open. A remarkable competitor.

***

My most memorable Hewitt match has got to be the Davis Cup match against Federer in Australia where Federer was killing him and he came back and won. He broke Federer's will by not going down. A personal memory was seeing him practice in Montreal in 2009 with Nathan Healey and how laser-like focused and intense he was in practice. It was like tunnel vision.   - Chris Chaffee

***

Hewitt always has been a regular on the practice courts during qualies before the U.S. Open. Sometimes if you spend the whole day there, you might catch Hewitt practicing a second time. One year I remember seeing Michael McClune destroy him in practice sets. I thought McClune   might have a future. - Harold Ashenberg

----

Chapter 9: Media & Insider Perspectives of Hewitt

David Mercer (EuroSport TV):   "My memories of Hewitt are of his total commitment. He is certainly not the most talented player to have been ranked number one in the world and won Grand Slam titles, but he has made the absolute most of his ability by always giving a hundred percent. He still does. I remember talking to Pat Rafter about Hewitt when Lleyton was first emerging on the Tour. He said, "He is the most competitive b.....d I have ever come across, who hates to lose at anything, whether it is tennis or tiddlywinks." Needless to say, Pat said it with a smile on his face."

Brad Gilbert (Coach, ESPN analyst and former ATP top five player):   "I coached against him with Roddick and Agassi, with Murray we didn't play him but we practiced with him quite a bit. We talked about him. Keep him in the middle of the court - make him create. Make him beat you with the forehand. Another thing I told Andre and Roddick when facing Hewitt - he has a great, little, sneaky serve out wide on the deuce court. He loves to serve wide on the deuce court to set up his point. He loves to do it on the second serve as well. His best serve is the one about 97 miles an hour wide. When he's on, that serve really sets up his first ball. When I was coaching against him I'd say you have to take that serve away from him, and force him to go up the middle...Make Hewitt try to be the aggressor. I feel he misses more in the middle of the court than by the doubles alley...A lot of counter punchers like Hewitt don't like when you give them no pace. That's when I think Hewitt struggles the most. Like Michael Chang, Hewitt is so effective on the run. When he had to create, he wasn't as good. Hewitt at his best is when he's creating on the run, great slices, he's more dangerous with his groundstrokes when he's in trouble, he gets more acceleration with his swing."

Ashley Fisher (Former ATP Pro and Tennis Channel analyst):   "I'll tell you about Lleyton Hewitt's professionalism. He was being coached by Joshua Eagle a few years ago, before the San Jose indoor swing. Eagle, who was Davis Cup coach for Australia, knew he was going to be late meeting Hewitt in San Jose. He emailed Lleyton to book a court that Friday night before San Jose. Hewitt responded, It's okay mate, I've already booked the court, I'm practicing with Verdasco. TWO weeks in advance, Hewitt already had the practice booked in San Jose. That's how professional Lleyton Hewitt is about his business."

"Nobody loves competing like Lleyton Hewitt. He loves the battle, he embraces it. He's going to struggle with retirement because of the passion he has for playing. But it won't take long for him to transition into a role with Tennis Australia. I imagine he'll be Davis Cup captain quite quickly."

"He's a person who really loves support and energy, he feeds off from support from his box."

John Skelly (Former coach of Vince Spadea):   "Vince could beat Federer, Sampras, Agassi, Kafelnikov, Nadal,

Safin, Roddick but he couldn't beat Lleyton Hewitt."

Clive Brunskill (Getty Images Photographer): "My first memory of Lleyton was winning the Adelaide Open, his first tournament. And then the one that stuck out in my mind was when he won the first Queens Club on grass. Then you thought: Oohh, he could win Wimbledon. Interesting."

Question: Lasting memory of Hewitt?

Clive Brunskill: "I've shot him for the last four or five years for the ATP campaign which we do in Indian Wells and I've shot him this year in March in Indian Wells. And he was great, he's a professional, he just gets it done in the studio. He's a tough guy. He's good, good fun."

Question: You've photographed all the greats of the modern era, how does Hewitt compare as a photography subject?

Clive Brunskill: "Hewitt's always great. Because Hewitt always gives his great celebrations. He was the one that started the big celebration. The big Come On, you know. On the court, he's really in your face as a player. As a photographer we always get great images of him. And he's just a great player. As time's gone on and things have changed, the top players have become Nadal, Federer...Hewitt was in that batch really just before that, in a way. And he had that gap when he was blowing everybody away. And then the game progresses a bit maybe the guys get a little stronger or faster. The younger Rafas come on and they were the next generation. But Hewitt still, to me, lives in that generation as one of the all time greats."

Question: Can you share a Hewitt story?

Clive Brunskill: "I've done Davis Cup and everything with him. The memorable thing to me is his Davis Cup wins when they went down to Nice ('99), Melbourne (vs. Spain in 2003), how many did he win? (Two.)   I remember two clearly. He's a generally good guy, always been nice to me, so..."

Jeff Burke (USA Today Photographer):   "Hewitt's always been fun to shoot because he's so expressive. Everytime he does something and he's been playing forever. Whether it's the first point or the last point he always works hard. And he always has a lot of energy and expression."

Question: Most memorable Hewitt matches?

Jeff Burke: "The funny thing is - any Lleyton Hewitt match, whether he wins or loses. You can't tell because he's always into it. He never tanks a point. He never gives up."

Question: Were you at his 600th career ATP singles match win in Miami vs. Robin Haase, a three-setter?

Jeff Burke: "Yes. That was a fun one. That, plus the fact he wears cool shirts, bright colors."

Allistair McCaw (Sports Performance Specialist & Consultant, Bradenton, FL):   "I have always admired Lleyton Hewitt and respected his attitude and fighting spirit. He has a game where he has to grind away, so fitness and mental toughness are key factors to his success. I've met him a few times, and even when you speak to him or see him in a restaurant or hotel he is still so intense. In a good way. But it's his personality. I know having worked with Bernard (Tomic), he has a lot of respect for him. If Bernard learns and takes the leaf out of Lleyton's book, it will be a huge difference in Bernie's game. But all good things take time. Lleyton definitely will go down in my top five favorite players because of his fighting spirit and his 'use it or lose it' mentality. I always like to use players like Lleyton Hewitt as an example to young kids. I feel he really did maximize his potential."

Pascal Maria (ATP Chair Umpire): "He is a great player and a great guy off the court."

Vince Spadea Sr. (Coach): "Very first tournament in Adelaide and (my son) Vince went to Adelaide to play. And Andre Agassi was there, he wanted to get an early start, he'd never played Adelaide. Vince played Nicolas Kiefer in the first match - a very tough match. Then he played Slava Dosedel in the second round - another top player back then. And Vince won that match. So here he is, through a very difficult part of the draw, into the quarterfinal. Now he's playing a young kid. Wildcard, first tournament in Adelaide, Australia. I watched him play. He had a really solid game. So they get on the court - Vince wins the first set. And then Lleyton never missed a ball. Lleyton's game was really consistent, all week when I watched him he never hit a ball over the baseline."

"One thing I said to Vince is sometimes Hewitt would chip the backhand return - you gotta take that chip away and get on top of the net to put it away. But in those days Vince was too young, he didn't do it. Lleyton won the second set. Long match and Lleyton ended up winning 7-5 in the third. It was really a good match. So the next day we were having breakfast at the player hotel. And Brad Gilbert comes down by himself - Andre had won that night before - Gilbert said, 'Hey what happened? What happened coach?' Back then, Brad didn't have a great appreciation for me as a coach. 'What happened? You choked.' He made the choke gesture.

'You should have beat that kid easy. You come out today and watch Andre give that kid a tennis lesson.'"

"Then Lleyton won 76 76 over Andre Agassi. Andre didn't even win a set. I waited for Brad at the hotel that night, to come back. But he never came. I never saw him again at his hotel. Somebody said they didn't even come back, they went straight to Melbourne. So that's a true story. Some tennis lesson, huh [smiles]?"

Christopher Clarey (Journalist for International Herald Tribune and The New York Times):   "Hewitt was playing Cedric Pioline at the Australian Open (first round). Hewitt took Pioline apart (63 61 61 in 1999).   It reminded me of how Andy Murray took apart Roddick at Wimbledon. Just took him apart, hit everthing back. Roddick threw his best stuff at him, Murray just had a vision and he just couldn't miss a return. And that was the kind of match Hewitt played with Pioline, who was a great player at the time. Everything Pioline tried, Hewitt was returning everything. And that's when I first said to myself: This guy is definitely going to win majors and be number one. And I would have never thought that until that match."

Question: What is your first memory of Hewitt?

Christopher Clarey: "I went to watch the match at U.S. Open qualies because he had won that tournament in Adelaide and I wanted to see him play. And he was just a complete and utter nightmare with a temper, raw anger unable to control himself - smashing racquets, swearing like a longshoreman, going crazy, you know, the whole thing. And you could just see this rage in him. And this burning desire to win. Other players have had that along the way too, and it's funny, maybe those are the guys that end up lasting longer sometimes. Really having that rage and then they end up containing it over a long career which may be part of the reason why that internal flame in him is glowing at a welder's level at this point. And I remember thinking: What a nightmare he must be to coach. And to play him was so tough because he was so crazed. But he was so quick. And a complete and utter terrier. Whoever coached him during this period helped him get a grip. He was much worse than Murray."

Question: Did Hewitt win or lose? Who was the opponent?

Christopher Clarey: "I remember he lost it.   In more ways than one. I think it was against Christophe Huet or Stephane Robert, you'll have to check."

Question: A lasting memory or anecdote of Hewitt?

Christopher Clarey: "I've interviewed him a few times. He's a guy who's much better as he's gotten older. His edges have gotten rounder. I think he understands the way the media works. I think he's somebody who is really, truly himself and if he really gave you all his insight, he'd be terrific, but I don't think he ever let go completely with the media. In a setting like this it's very rare. And I also think he was also kind of dealing with everybody, on the outside of his camp, as an adversary. And I think he still does, to some degree. It's that 'Aussie Rules' thing he grew up with. Even though the Aussie Rules guys can be engaging, there's a kind of warrior mentality that goes there: Either you're part of the guild, or you're not. But I think he's a terrific TV commentator."

Chapter 10:   Miscellaneous Hewitt

Lleyton Hewitt's 5-set record is 32-19:

1998 Australian Open R128: Daniel Vacek def. Lleyton
Hewitt (6-2, 6-4, 1-6, 2-6, 6-3)
1999 French Open R128: Martin Rodriguez def. Lleyton
Hewitt (4-6, 6-4, 6-4, 4-6, 6-4)
1999 US Open R32: Andrei Medvedev def. Lleyton Hewitt
(3-6, 6-3, 3-6, 6-4, 6-3)
2000 French Open R64: Lleyton Hewitt def. Markus
Hantschk (2-6, 6-3, 3-6, 6-2, 6-3)
2000 Stuttgart Indoor F: Wayne Ferreira def. Lleyton
Hewitt (7-6, 3-6, 6-7, 7-6, 6-2)
2000 Davis Cup F: Lleyton Hewitt def. Albert Costa (3-6,
6-1, 2-6, 6-4, 6-4)
2001 Australian Open R128: Lleyton Hewitt def. Jonas
Bjorkman (7-5, 4-6, 2-6, 6-3, 6-2)
2001 Australian Open R32: Carlos Moya def. Lleyton
Hewitt (4-6, 6-1, 5-7, 6-2, 7-5)
2001 French Open R16: Lleyton Hewitt def. Guillermo
Canas (3-6, 6-7, 6-2, 6-3, 6-3)
2001 Wimbledon R64: Lleyton Hewitt def. Taylor Dent

(1-6, 7-5, 6-3, 6-7, 6-3)

2001 Wimbledon R16: Nicolas Escude def. Lleyton Hewitt (4-6, 6-4, 6-3, 4-6, 6-4)

2001 US Open R64: Lleyton Hewitt def. James Blake (6-4, 3-6, 2-6, 6-3, 6-0)

2001 US Open QF: Lleyton Hewitt def. Andy Roddick (6-7, 6-3, 6-4, 3-6, 6-4)

2001 Davis Cup F: Nicolas Escude def. Lleyton Hewitt (4-6, 6-3, 3-6, 6-3, 6-4)

2002 Wimbledon QF: Lleyton Hewitt def. Sjeng Schalken (6-2, 6-2, 6-7, 1-6, 7-5)

2002 US Open R32: Lleyton Hewitt def. James Blake (6-7, 6-3, 6-4, 3-6, 6-3)

2002 Masters Cup F: Lleyton Hewitt def. Juan Carlos Ferrero (7-5, 7-5, 2-6, 2-6, 6-4)

2003 Australian Open R128: Lleyton Hewitt def. Magnus Larsson (6-3, 3-6, 6-1, 6-7, 6-2)

2003 French Open R32: Tommy Robredo def. Lleyton Hewitt (4-6, 1-6, 6-3, 6-2, 6-3)

2003 Davis Cup SF: Lleyton Hewitt def. Roger Federer (5-7, 2-6, 7-6, 7-5, 6-1)

2003 Davis Cup F: Lleyton Hewitt def. Juan Carlos Ferrero (3-6, 6-3, 3-6, 7-6, 6-2)

2004 French Open R32: Lleyton Hewitt def. Martin Verkerk (6-2, 3-6, 4-6, 6-2, 6-1)

2005 Australian Open R16: Lleyton Hewitt def. Rafael Nadal (7-5, 3-6, 1-6, 7-6, 6-2)

2005 Australian Open QF: Lleyton Hewitt def. D. Nalbandian (6-3, 6-2, 1-6, 3-6, 10-8)

2005 US Open R32: Lleyton Hewitt def. Taylor Dent (6-3, 3-6, 6-7, 6-2, 7-5)

2005 US Open QF: Lleyton Hewitt def. Jarkko Nieminen (2-6, 6-1, 3-6, 6-3, 6-1)

2006 Australian Open R128: Lleyton Hewitt def. Robin Vik (6-4, 2-6, 5-7, 7-6, 6-3)

2006 Wimbledon R64: Lleyton Hewitt def. Hyung-Taik Lee (6-7, 6-2, 7-6, 6-7, 6-4)

2006 US Open R16: Lleyton Hewitt def. Richard Gasquet (6-4, 6-4, 4-6, 3-6, 6-3)

2006 Davis Cup SF: Jose Acasuso def. Lleyton Hewitt (1-6, 6-4, 4-6, 6-2, 6-1)

2007 Australian Open R128: Lleyton Hewitt def. Michael Russell (3-6, 2-6, 6-3, 6-3, 6-3)

2007 Davis Cup 1R: Kristof Vliegen def. Lleyton Hewitt (4-6, 6-4, 3-6, 6-3, 6-4)

2007 Davis Cup 1R: Lleyton Hewitt def. Olivier Rochus (6-2, 6-3, 6-7, 3-6, 6-1)

2007 French Open R64: Lleyton Hewitt def. Gaston Gaudio (4-6, 3-6, 6-2, 6-4, 6-2)

2007 Davis Cup: Lleyton Hewitt def. Janko Tipsarevic (6-2, 3-6, 4-6, 6-1, 6-1)

2008 Australian Open R32: Lleyton Hewitt def. M. Baghdatis (4-6, 7-5, 7-5, 6-7, 6-3)

2008 French Open R32: David Ferrer def. Lleyton Hewitt (6-2, 3-6, 3-6, 6-3, 6-4)

2008 Wimbledon R128: Lleyton Hewitt def. Robin Haase (6-7, 6-3, 6-3, 6-7, 6-2)

2009 Australian Open R128: Fer. Gonzalez def. Lleyton Hewitt (5-7, 6-2, 6-2, 3-6, 6-3)

2009 Davis Cup: Danai Udomchoke def. Lleyton Hewitt (2-6, 4-6, 7-6, 6-4, 6-1)

2009 French Open R128: Lleyton Hewitt def. Ivo Karlovic (6-7, 6-7, 7-6, 6-4, 6-3)

2009 Wimbledon R16: Lleyton Hewitt def. Radek Stepanek (4-6, 2-6, 6-1, 6-2, 6-2)

2009 Wimbledon QF: Andy Roddick def. Lleyton Hewitt (6-3, 6-7, 7-6, 4-6, 6-4)

2010 French Open R64: Lleyton Hewitt def. Denis Istomin (1-6, 6-3, 6-4, 2-6, 6-2)

2010 US Open R128: Paul-Henri Mathieu def. Lleyton

Hewitt (6-3, 6-4, 5-7, 4-6, 6-1)

2011 Australian Open R128: D. Nalbandian def. Lleyton Hewitt (3-6, 6-4, 3-6, 7-6, 9-7)

2011 Wimbledon R64: Robin Soderling def. Lleyton Hewitt (6-7, 3-6, 7-5, 6-4, 6-4)

2011 Davis Cup: Stanislas Wawrinka def. Lleyton Hewitt (4-6, 6-4, 6-7, 6-4, 6-3)

2012 US Open R64: Lleyton Hewitt def. Gilles Muller (3-6, 7-6, 6-7, 7-5, 6-4)

2013 French Open R128: Gilles Simon def. Lleyton Hewitt (3-6, 1-6, 6-4, 6-1, 7-5)

2013 US Open R64 Lleyton Hewitt def. JM Del Potro (6-4, 5-7, 3-6, 7-6, 6-1)

2014 Australian Open R128: Andreas Seppi def. Lleyton Hewitt (7-6, 6-3, 5-7, 5-7, 7-5)

DOB: February 24, 1981

Birthplace: Adelaide, Australia

Turned Pro: 1998

Height: 5-11

Weight: 170 pounds

Highest ATP Doubles Ranking: 18 in 2000.

Record vs. Number One Ranked Players: 0-18.

Residence: Nassau, Bahamas.

Record in Masters Series Finals: 2-5 (won Indian Wells

in 2002, 2003, lost Cincinnati in 2002, 2004 and Paris Indoors 2002)

First ATP singles title: Adelaide 1998.

First ATP singles title in America: Delray Beach 1999.

First ATP singles title in Asia: Tokyo 2001.

Youngest player in ATP history to achieve the number one ranking (20 years and eight months) in 2001. (Second-youngest was Marat Safin (20 years and nine months in 2000).

Olympics Record: 3-3 (First round in Sydney 2000, Second round Beijing 2008, Third round London 2012).

Clothing/Shoe Endorsers: Previously, Nike shoes and clothing, Yonex racquets. Then Yonex clothing and shoes. Currently, Athletic DNA clothing, Yonex shoes and Yonex racquets.

Historical Fact: Lleyton Hewitt is the only player to win a Grand Slam major singles title   (2001 U.S. Open), while wearing his cap backwards.

List of players since Hewitt won the 2001 U.S. Open, who wear/have worn their cap backwards:

Michael Lammer

Mischa Zverev

Illya Marchenko

Paul-Henri Mathieu

Ruben Ramirez Hidalgo

Tim Smyczek

Jack Sock

Martina Navratilova

Frank Dancevic

Jarmere Jenkins

Taro Daniel

Vahid Mirzadeh

Benjamin Becker

Tommy Haas

John Isner

Richard Gasquet

James Cerretani

Rafael Nadal (in practice)

Roger Federer (in practice)

Carlos Moya

Albert Montanes

Gilles Simon

Robby Ginepri

Jan-Lennard Struff

Jurgen Melzer

Andreas Seppi

Denis Kudla

Ricardas Berankis

Rainer Schuettler

Alex Bogomolov

Juan Ignacio Chela

Rhyne Williams

Somdev Devvarman

Paolo Lorenzi

Guillermo Coria

Bernard Tomic

Lukasz Kubot

Nicolas Kiefer

Andrei Pavel

Sebastien Grosjean

Joao Sousa

Kei Nishikori

Jerzy Janowicz

Go Soeda

Matthew Ebden

Kevin Anderson

Andy Roddick

Chapter 11   - Facing Hewitt

"He's really, really an unbelievable tennis player."

Goran Ivanisevic: "I actually played him once. I lost the last tennis match in my career against Lleyton in the most beautiful center court in the world, Wimbeldon. He just beat me pretty badly. Lleyton is one of the best tennis players, ever, unbelievable, great fighter. That's the guy who plays till the last, last point. So, that was a great experience for me. I don't mind that of my last match, of my career, that I lost to Lleyton Hewitt. That's a pretty good honor for me. Even if I lost, it's nice."

Question: Did anything surprise you about him?

Goran Ivanisevic: "Nothing surprises me. He was really very tough. He has everything. He can play on all surfaces. He's really, really an unbelievable tennis player. He's great. One of the best fighters, best return of serve guys in the history of tennis."

Question: Last match of your career. That had to be a special moment?

Goran Ivanisevic: "Last match of my career, center court, Wimbledon."

Question: Do you have a lasting memory or anecdote of Lleyton Hewitt?

Goran Ivanisevic: "He kicked my ass [smiles]. When he came I was already done. So we didn't play so many times. So, like I said, one time. But I watch a lot of his matches and he's really impressive. Nice guy to watch."

Hewitt leads series   3-0

2000	Queens	R16	Hewitt 64 64
2001	s'-Hertogenbosch	R16	Hewitt 64 75
2004	Wimbledon	R32	Hewitt 62 63 64

"I just walked off the court and Lleyton thought it was funny."

Alex Bogomolov Jr.:   "I remember my first first memory was obviously when he crashed onto the scene. I remember him in Adelaide when he was sixteen years old, just hearing about this new kid. He was winning ATP matches at sixteen years old. And then my personal memory was I played him - I got a wildcard at Cincinnati when I was nineteen years old, into the Masters Series right before the U.S. Open. I played him first round. He was the first seed there. He was number one in the world then. And I remember it was in the middle of the day. Hot as anything and we played, just battled first set 6-4. And after that I started only serve and volleying because I was dead. The guy just... I always admired his conditioning... he took care of himself so well. And even now, to come back from all the injuries. My main memory was thinking: Man, to beat this guy you have to keep like fifty balls in play every single point."

Question: Did anything surprise you about Hewitt?

Alex Bogomolov Jr.: "To tell you the truth, the whole incident at U.S. Open was a little surprising, because he played James Blake. I just know that it was competitive nature. I don't think it was necessarily anything racist or anything. Just the outbursts... I know it was a tight match. I remember reading or even looking at it and I didn't really expect that at that time."

Question: It seemed to be way overblown.

Alex Bogomolov Jr.: "Yeah, the whole thing. I felt like Lleyton and James have mutual respect for each other. And it was heat of the moment. And it was overblown. Of course, it was at the U.S. Open."

Question: You played against Hewitt just that one time?

Alex Bogomolov Jr.: "I played him that one time. Actually, I don't think I've played him since. We practiced together a couple of times. I practiced with him at Rod Laver Arena for like two straight days for the Australian Open a couple of years back. We practiced for like two hours. I remember I got a phone call at the hotel, from the tournament director, that Lleyton wanted to practice tomorrow morning. Are you available? Yes, of course."

Question: Another player told me Hewitt practices so hard that they didn't stop for a water break for forty minutes. Was there anything memorable for you practicing with Hewitt?

Alex Bogomolov Jr.:   "We just went straight into... I don't like doing cross courts so much. I grew up doing that with my dad. I was kinda dreading the whole beginning of the practice. I was surprised because we went straight into baseline games, which I love. I don't remember if he asked me or if I asked first. Baseline games? And we ended up playing like four or five of them like back to back. Like up to fifteen. In the heat. It was great, great practice."

Question: Do you have any kind of rapport or interaction with Hewitt?

Alex Bogomolov Jr.:   "After the Cincinnati match when we were shaking hands, I was young and I admired his game and I said something like, 'You're my favorite player' or something, whatever. I was nineteen [smiles]. I think since then we always said Hi to each other. We talk in the locker room if there's a specific core area to talk about. We talked about my incident in Chicago, where I walked off the court, the umpire was cheating me. And I just walked off the court. And Lleyton thought it was funny. He said he always wanted to do that but never did [smiles]."

Question: Lasting memory of Hewitt, on or off court?

Alex Bogomolov Jr.:   "Well, I think for me, I always take how the transition from the kid who burst on the scene, long hair, fighting and Come On and not caring what anybody was thinking... into a family man who is still doing the exact same thing, fighting for every point. Two or three kids. And still doing what he loves at this age. For me, to see him then, to see him now, is kinda cool. Because I'm also thirty years old and I've seen it all. The whole process, dealing with injuries, everything. I'll say that."

Hewitt leads series   1-0

2004   Cincinnati Masters   R64   Hewitt 62 64

"You cannot for one second feel like now I can slow down or maybe I step back a little bit."

Yen-Hsun Lu: "He's a guy who's fighting on every ball. You don't expect he'll give you any free points. You always have to put in all the energy to win every point, every rally, and also it's difficult, you cannot for one second feel like now I can slow down or maybe I step back a little bit. You always have to keep the same level against this guy because this guy is always standing there fighting every point. So I think this is the feeling when you go out there to play him. I always feel it in this way."

Question: What was your most memorable match with Hewitt?

Yen-Hsun Lu: "I played him - I'm not quite sure, four or

five times. We always have close matches. Last time I lost to him in Memphis and I was up a set and I had the chance to break and go into 6-5 serving and I didn't make it. The funniest thing is we always have to have long rallies and to make a lot of effort to win the point. Even though you know the kind of game he plays it's still difficult [smiles]. You know you need to do something to play better than him. I respect him very much. I like to play him. But other times I don't like to play him. First of all he gives me the rhythms from the baseline because he's always putting the ball back, rally is good. He doesn't kill you from the first ball. So you can get good rhythm. But you still need to work really hard, to break his rhythm or to make extra speed to make a point. This is always the way you have to play him. Every match I always remember in this way."

Question: Lasting memory of Hewitt?

Yen-Hsun Lu: "Actually, I just know him when I start to play him. And even more then. I think he changed a little bit after he dropped in the ranking but also coming back from injuries. I feel he's relaxing a little more than before. When he was ranked in the top twenty you can feel he want it a lot. Even now he still want it but it looks like he enjoys it more, to play during the tournament. And also, he has the young boy, the kids, when he's practicing with his boy he's running on the court. Last week in Memphis I asked him, I was missing his boy, I hope to see him again. When he's still playing in the tournament. He's a nice guy."

Question: You beat Hewitt, how did you do it?

Yen-Hsun Lu: "I beat him two times, he beat me also I think two times. You have to get his habit. He has one corner he normally likes to play down the line or cross. You can try and get this, then you're a little bit one step ahead of him because you know where he goes. Then, easily, you can do something, changing and going to the net. Or maybe speed up the speed of the shot. So this is always what I try to change when I play him. So that's why I think this is a key point why I beat him two times."

Hewitt leads series 3-2

2009   Delray Beach   R32   Lu   75 26 62
2010   Cincinnati   R64   Hewitt   64 40 ret.
2011   Memphis   R 32   Hewitt 64 76
2011   Indian Wells Masters   R128   Lu 62 63

2013   Memphis   R32   Hewitt   26 76 64

"His return has given me fits."

John Isner: "Yeah, it's tough to play Hewitt, his return is one of the best. It's given me fits in the past. He's beaten me more times than I've beaten him."

Hewitt leads series 4-2

2009   Shanghai Masters   R64 Hewitt 62 64
2010   World Team Championship Dusseldorf   RR Hewitt 62 64
2012   Newport   F   Isner   76 64
2013   Indian Wells Masters   R64   Hewitt   67 63 64
2013   Newport   SF   Hewitt 57 62 64

2013   Atlanta   SF   Isner 64 46 76

"He just embarrassed me."

Bob Bryan: "Well, I was lucky enough to play him in singles and doubles. I think I played him when he was number one. I qualified that week. I think it was Montreal and I was feeling good about my chances. Maybe I didn't think I was gonna take him but I thought I'd have a very competitive match with him. He just embarrassed me [smiles]. He was taking the ball so early. And just giving me no free points at all. He was picking up every one of my serves and had me on my toes. That's really the worst that I've ever been beaten on the Tour. And it was at the hands of Lleyton. So I have great respect for him and we've played him a lot in the doubles and he's no easy out. He returns that backhand in the ad court as well as or better than anyone out there. And he's an underrated volleyer. I mean, he can really dig out the tough, shoelace volley and hit it crosscourt. Obviously, he never gives a bad effort. Some singles players - after a tough day at the office - might mail it in in doubles. You never get that feeling that Lleyton ever didn't compete at his fullest."

Question: Did anything surprise you about him?

Bob Bryan: "I was in college when he got on the Tour. Watched him a million times on TV. He's a very nice guy. I wouldn't say he's a super open guy, not a guy you're going to have a lot of conversations with in the players' lounge. He stays close to his team, which you respect. He's a great competitor. I don't know if he lets a lot of people in. But I have a lot of respect for the guy."

Question: Lasting memory or anecdote of Lleyton Hewitt?

Bob Bryan: "Just all the matches we've played have been doubles, it's always been in front of a packed house. So though he's number one thirteen or fourteen years ago, he still has a huge following and every time I faced him, it didn't matter where it is in the world, he had a lot of Lleyton Hewitt fans there supporting him."

Hewitt leads series 1-0

2003   Montreal Masters   R64   Hewitt 62 62

"He's a legend. And one of my idols."

Rhyne Williams: "Well, he's a legend. And one of my idols. It was a sweet experience to play him and we had a nice match. From what I remember, I had my chances but he's just too good."

Question: Does your wearing your hat backwards have anything to do with paying respects to Hewitt?

Rhyne Williams: "No, not really. I've done it my whole life. I don't know, it's kind of my thing. It's a lot of people's thing. I've been doing it since I was nine years old."

Question: Did anything surprise you when you played Hewitt?

Rhyne Williams: "I would say the speed of his serve, he really mixes it up. I remember him using a slider serve, like almost every time. And it was sort of predictable but it was also really tricky because it was really low and really hard to adjust to."

Question: Slider out wide deuce court?

Rhyne Williams: "All day."

Hewitt leads series   1-0

2013   Atlanta   R16   Hewitt 76 64

"He never looks like there's a lack of motivation."

Raven Klassen: "I played Hewitt only in doubles. First round this year in Australia with Pat Rafter. It was probably one of the most exciting matches of my career. We got on Hi Sense Arena early and played against two legends of the game. That was very nervous and exciting for us. So happy to get the win there (Klassen and partner Eric Butorac proceeded to make the Australian Open finals where they were defeated by Kubot/Lindstedt.)

Question: How did that match vs. Hewitt/Rafter play out?

Raven Klassen: "Well, obviously the start was just try to be prepared for a hostile crowd. We knew the crowd didn't want us to win. We also knew that there were two guys that had so much success in the sport. And Lleyton just played in singles the day before (losing in five sets to Andreas Seppi) so we knew he was going to be seeing the ball well. But for us, we knew we had been playing good tennis, let's concentrate on that and what we need to do well. Because if they play to their level, they're going to be tough to beat. These guys have done so much. I don't think there's any match in my life that I was more excited to get out there. Really exciting match."

Question: Were there any surprises about playing Lleyton for the first time?

Raven Klassen: "What amazes me more than anything after all the years, he's still such a fighter. He never looks like there's a lack of motivation. I think as guys get older, and their career progresses, they kind of lose that fire. And he looks like it's just day one for him. So he still has so much guts. And he's still pulling out matches where you think perhaps he shouldn't be winning. When you watch that sort of guts and fight, it really inspires you to try and get a little more out of yourself."

Question: Lasting memory of Hewitt?

Raven Klassen: "I think Hewitt is one of the first guys to really get the positive self going. He gave the big Come Ons when he was younger. When he'd win a point and really get the crowd going. I think that fire really stood out for me when I watched him early. To be as good as he was at such an early age, he really had to back himself against some of these bigger players. Because he went toe to toe with Sampras in his prime. With Agassi in his prime. And he got the better of them. So when I look at how much passion and fight he has for this game... he leaves nothing out there."

Question: Every talk or interact with him?

Raven Klassen: "Unfortunately, I don't get to hang out with Lleyton that much. But we'll occasionally greet if we walk by. And you see him a lot in the locker room. At the moment, he kind of has his family and crew around him. But he greets when I walk by, but no real communication."

"He's been playing sixteen years now, his practice sessions seem like he's still trying to come up."

Benjamin Becker: "I played him on grass in the semifinals of Halle. I was playing quite well, confident. I won the first set 7-6 and then I lost 6-4 or 6-3 in the third set. I remember I lost the second set tiebreaker. It was a close match. The memories of the match are it being so different than everybody else. He's playing very flat, every ball really stays very low. Because there's not really much to do, instead of hitting it, you need to really hit it up. And his serve also stays very flat. He doesn't miss. He moves very well. He doesn't miss. He's very balanced, always. So he's a very tough player to play against. You don't really see from the outside how tough it is to play him. He really makes you work hard for every point."

Question: What is your first memory of Hewitt?

Benjamin Becker: "Reading a newspaper when I was sixteen and he was sixteen. He won the tournament in Adelaide. As a sixteen year old. I can't believe that somebody my age can win an ATP tournament. And that was my first memory. Then, obviously, watching him get to number one in the world and winning two Grand Slams. Obviously an unbelievable competitor. Always on fire. Always 100% no matter what the score is."

Question: Did you ever practice together?

Benjamin Becker: "I did practice with him a few times. Played doubles against him in Davis Cup. I hit a couple of times with him. I remember in Atlanta. He seems like a very nice guy. But also in practice he's very intense. He's been playing sixteen years now, his practice sessions seem like he's still trying to come up...still a youngster and trying to come up. Which is pretty impressive."

Question: Lasting memory or anecdote of Hewitt?

Benjamin Becker: "He's very friendly. We talk a little bit when we see each other. Obviously we played Davis Cup in the doubles. It was a big match for us. We spent a little bit of time together. For me, obviously, it's a bad memory, losing to him in Davis Cup in four sets in Germany, which would have been a 2-1 for Germany. But still, it would have been nice to get the win there. He was the best player on the court. And really dominating the doubles. And yeah, that's what he's done the last sixteen years."

Question: You lost to him in Halle and Davis Cup, any other matches?

Benjamin Becker: "Oh, and I lost to him in Cincinnati.

Quite easily actually, 2007 or 2008, where he just played too good for me."

Question: If Hewitt and Nadal trade bodies and physical strengths, who do you think would be the better player?

Benjamin Becker: "It's really tough to compare. It seems like Nadal needs his muscle and strength to play the game he plays. Hewitt doesn't need to be that strong on the outside. But he's, as I said, very balanced, very good with his legs. And very quick. So the way it worked out for them, it was very good. I think with the body of Nadal, it would be tough for him to play as smooth as he did. And Nadal - he needs the strength, he needs the racquet head speed. And Hewitt is a small guy, he uses his legs and his core - the counter puncher - to get his strength to the opponent."

Hewitt leads series 2-0

| 2009 | Cincinnati Masters | R32 | Hewitt 63 63 |
| 2010 | Halle | SF | Hewitt 67 76 62 |

"He can make any shot on the court."

Santiago Gonzalez: "I played against Hewitt twice, in Atlanta last year and Delray Beach this year. It's always a tough match against him, he's a former number one, very good player. It's fun to try to beat him in doubles."

Question: Did anything surprise you about playing Hewitt?

Santiago Gonzalez: "He's a very good returner. In the doubles you need to be ready in every single point against him. He can make any shot on the court."

Question: What was memorable about competing against Hewitt on court?

Santiago Gonzalez: "Just the way he hit the ball - flat. He's so close to the net. It's tough to return every single ball."

Question: What is your first memory of Hewitt?

Santiago Gonzalez: "When he won Wimbledon like ten years ago."

Question: Watching on TV as a kid?

Santiago Gonzalez: "Not as a kid. I'm 30 years old [smiles]. I was playing out there and trying to be a professional, in the Futures, maybe I was in qualies of Wimbledon. So it's fun now to play against him."

Question: Lasting memory of Hewitt from the tournament?

Santiago Gonzalez: "We played yesterday. He's playing the singles here, he wants to focus on singles. He wants to keep trying to be number one."

Question: How did you and Scott Lipsky beat Hewitt and Chris Guccione yesterday?

Santiago Gonzalez: "We had to play our best tennis to beat him. With the shadows and the sun in the court it was kind of difficult for the four of us. But at the end we were lucky to get the tiebreak and we got the win."

Question: Did you win both times?

Santiago Gonzalez: "No, we lost in Atlanta. It was kind of revenge. We got the same partners, we lost in super tiebreak in Atlanta and we won here in super-breaker. So we're one-all. I hope we can play him again."

Question: Did you change tactics at all?

Santiago Gonzalez: "Maybe play a little more to the partner. Between Guccione, Hewitt is the better player on the court so we try to play the other side of the court more. So I think we do this. And it worked out for us."

"It took forty minutes to have a drink of water."

Alejandro Falla: "I play him in Washington DC. It was unfortunate the way I won. It's tough to play him because he's such a fighter and such a great competitor. It's tough because you know you have to run so much on the court. But it's also nice because you play long rallies. I like that way to play. We practice together also a few times. I always have to be mentally prepared for battle against Hewitt."

Question: What do you remember about your match with Hewitt?

Alejandro Falla: "We play in Washington DC. We play the third set. He had to retire. It was unfortunate.

Unfortunately I couldn't end the match the way I wanted to. That was the only time we played. It was a very tough match, over a hundred degrees on court. And we were running so much. Playing really long rallies. We both return pretty good. There were a lot of rallies."

Question: What tactics did you use that were successful against Hewitt?

Alejandro Falla: "We play similar, we both are counterpunchers. We both have a good backhand. The match was hard. It could have gone either way. But he had to retire, that's why I won it. I was playing well. It was play to his forehand, which is his worst shot...not his worst but his backhand is much better. But I was trying to attack his forehand and put some pressure on him. But also play with him. Play long rallies. But I have to be mentally prepared to run a lot."

Question: Do you have a lasting memory of Hewitt?

Alejandro Falla: "A practice I remember last year in San Jose. We practiced for like an hour and it took me like forty minutes to have a changeover and have some water [smiles]. Amazing. He is so intense the way he practices. He doesn't waste time by sitting and drinking water.   It took forty minutes to have a drink of water...so I remember that."

Question: I saw you practiced with Hewitt today (in Delray Beach), how did it go today?

Alejandro Falla: "Yes, we played a couple of sets. We played for two hours. I won the first set 6-1 and then he was leading the second set. It was a very good practice. I think it's a pleasure playing against him. Because he's a very good competitor and he fights a lot. And he's a very good guy."

Series tied 1-1

| 2004 | Washington DC | R16 | Hewitt | 63 62 | |
| 2007 | Washington DC | R32 | Falla | 75 32 | ret. |

"He's making his shots every time...that's his pressure."

Tomasz Bednarek: "He's a great player with a great history. What can I say about his strokes... for sure he is a very solid player. So he's putting every return in on the second serve, basically. He puts pressure on your serve. He's not playing the ball fast. He cannot hit that good. But he's making his shots every time so that's his pressure. So you have to win the point, basically."

Question: Was there anything that Hewitt did that surprised you?

Tomasz Bednarek: "In Memphis last week, like I said, he makes no mistakes. He's making you play as many shots as possible. Great volleyer. With his returns he was always ready for the first volley. I saw him on TV before, I watched him on You Tube - some doubles matches. We were kind of ready for this. So, not really. Maybe the volleys. I thought maybe he doesn't have such a good reflex. He's pretty good at the volley."

"Lleyton Hewitt is a guy, you physically feel his intensity on the other side of the net."

Prakash Amritraj: "It was weird. Because I was on practice courts with him and I've been around him quite a bit. I knew the guy. He was always quite nice. But once he knew he was playing me, he became short. It's okay though, I understand. We played on center court in Newport, in the second round, in the afternoon, it was a nice, summer day. We were out on the court warming up and only when I heard the announcer say 'former number one, former Wimbledon and U.S. Open champion...' ...that's when it hit me I was playing Lleyton Hewitt. It was a little intimidating at that point. I think the biggest thing that stood out about him in the match was his intensity. It doesn't matter whoever he's playing, he's always at full intensity."

"I remember in the match I had a lot of chances to break him. The scoreline is deceiving. I remember in the first game of the match, he saved a break point. He managed to save it and he let out a fist pump and a Come On that I've never heard before. Four minutes into the match. I was kind of thrown a bit by that. I think he saved it on an error too, I missed a forehand crosscourt. It kind of hit me then again...I was playing Lleyton Hewitt. I was still in juniors when he was doing well in the ATP."

"But it's great to see that kind of passion. When I talk about tennis with people, I say it's about the process not the results. He personifies that how he's so into the battle. I think that's really a key to all of his success."

Question: Were you pleased with your performance vs. Hewitt?

Prakash Amritraj: "I was frustrated - for two reasons. I had like about eight games of 15-40 and love-40 which I didn't convert. It was ludicrous. Also, I had a little problem with my shoulder. I played him in the second round, the next day after my first round match (win over Flavio Cipolla) but my shoulder was a bit sore. I actually had surgery four weeks after that match. Everything was to my liking, playing him on grass, I just wasn't feeling as healthy as I would have liked."

Question: Lasting memory of playing Hewitt?

Prakash Amritraj: "Two things. The intensity, the ferocity he has to compete. The fist pump/yell in the first game. He's all about the old school, gunslinger swagger. He has that attitude, which I love. I think he's great for the sport, the fans love to see a player like him. I say this in a positive way: the swagger and confidence he has has carried him so far. He's overcome so much in his career."

"Another thing was his focus. The minute we both won our first round matches and we knew we were going to play each other, there was no more, Hi how are you. Even my dad (Vijay), who was with me in Newport, who has interviewed Lleyton so many times... Lleyton kind of looked the other way. Once he knew he was up against me and my team, he's straight focused, all business. His job is to come at you."

Question: Is Hewitt the most intense guy you ever played?

Prakash Amritraj: "Yes. Yes, I say so. It was the most that I physically felt the opponent's intensity. Lots of guys are very intense, they work so hard...Lleyton Hewitt is a guy, you physically feel his intensity on the other side of the net."

Hewitt leads series   1-0

2013   Newport R16   Hewitt 62 61

"I'll never forget that shot."

James Cerretani: "I played him in Houston, I want to say it was 2010. I was playing with my long-time friend and colleague Adil Shamasdin. We were playing against Lleyton and his coach at the time, Nathan Healey. They got a wildcard entry. So we thought that that might help us, playing a wildcard. But anytime you're playing Hewitt it's gonna be a tough battle. Healey, who was coaching him at the time, was about 150 at one point and top 50 in doubles. So we knew we were in for a tough match."

"We were serving for the first set. I was serving at 5-3. I think it was actually quadruple set point. I'm not really too proud about the story but [smiles] they came up with a few good shots. It got to deuce. I hit a real good first serve to Lleyton. Lleyton hit a forehand inside out return - he was playing ad-side. Then I made a real nice first volley deep in the backhand corner. And he slid, ever so elegantly, into the ball and kind of held it, at the last moment flicked a backhand topspin lob winner in classic Lleyton Hewitt fashion. To perfection. And curved it right over my head. Landed inside the baseline by about a foot for a clean winner. And that was that. Then it was a battle from there."

"They ended up winning. I think it was like 6 and 5 or something like that. I'll never forget that shot. That's my memory of playing Hewitt in doubles. He's a great player. You know he's gonna come up with a few shots. If you ask people who the best lobber is - he does so many things great - but one of the best lobbers of all time, I think Lleyton would be in that top five category. He really disguises it well and he used it to perfection on that point. And he's won a Grand Slam in doubles - he won the U.S. Open with Max Mirnyi."

Question: I just interviewed Rick Leach recently and he said Hewitt hit a perfect topspin lob in the third set tiebreak of their U.S. Open final that he said basically gave them the match.

James Cerretani: "It's definitely a difference maker. It's a reason why he's a champion. And he's able to come up with those shots at the most important times. Much to my dismay - and a lot of other players' dismay [smiles]. But he does it and he gets the crown. And he's really evolved into a class act too, over the course of his career. He's really a nice guy and I think that's the most important thing."

Question: Any memory or anecdote of Hewitt before the match, or off the court, which may capture his essence?

James Cerretani: "Really chill, nothing...kinda 'Hey, how you doing? Hey mate, what's goin' on?' Really friendly kind of Aussie vibe. I know a lot of Australians really quite well. I haven't really developed a personal relationship with Lleyton but we get on fine, when we see each other at events. And I think a lot of the Aussies have really good things to say about him. Especially as he's matured and evolved, like I said, later in his career. He's got his wife, kids. I think his perspective has changed a lot on life and the Tour, he's a good dude."

"He played a Japanese wildcard and he was so pumped up from the first point."

Frank Moser: "I played him twice in doubles, once in Wimbledon, once in San Jose. He's always one of the players I like to watch. Because I love his attitude and how he's fighting for every point. And when I play against him I just want to win, of course. But I respect him a lot and it's an honor to play against him."

Question: Who was your partner, who was his partner?

Frank Moser: "One time I played with Matthias Bachinger. And one time with Xavier Malisse. He played with Peter Luczak, who is coaching him now, part time at least. Other time Marinko Matosevic."

Question: Did anything about Hewitt surprise you?

Frank Moser: "Not when I played against him. I mean, he has very good lobs. His return is just ridiculous. I know there were some parts where I felt like I can't win points against him when I'm serving. Because he was returning really really good. And his ball comes really flat. More flat than other guys, especially on the backhand side. But there weren't really surprises. These are the kinds of things I expect already when I go on for the match."

Question: Did you win either of these matches?

Frank Moser: "Yeah, I won them both actually. WE won them both."

Question: Lasting memory or anecdote of Hewitt?

Frank Moser: "I think he's really a nice guy. I watched him play a long time ago when he was top five in the world, in Japan. He was playing against a Japanese wildcard. And the guy wasn't ranked that high... and Hewitt was so pumped up from the first point. He took the other guy super serious. I was there watching. That was 2002. It seemed to me like he took this guy as serious as if he was playing the number one in the world. That showed a good attitude."

"Actually it's not funny. He's intimidating."

Mischa Zverev: "I never played a match with him. We practiced a few times. Obviously he's a great player. What I remember from practicing with him... he's someone that would never miss. He would run down every single ball, even if it's practice. He was tough to beat whether it's a match or practice. He's like a Nadal type of player. A little bit older but he's a great player, he battles down every point. Very tough to play."

Question: Where was the practice at and when?

Mischa Zverev: "I think 2010 in the Australian Open."

Question: Did anything surprise you about him?

Mischa Zverev: "No not really. It was exactly what I expected of him. It was a tough practice."

Question: Do you have any kind of lasting memory or anecdote of Hewitt?

Mischa Zverev: "Everybody was, not making fun of him... everybody remembers him as a fist-pumping guy, yelling COME ON. Actually, it's not funny, he's intimidating. He's definitely a great character."

Question: Over the years I saw a few players imitate Hewitt's Come On in practice, like Todd Martin at U.S. Open on Ashe Stadium years ago. It sounded exactly like Hewitt so it was very funny.

Mischa Zverev: "Some guys like to do that in practice, joke around a little bit. Lleyton is definitely a great player, you're okay imitating him. He's not just like a random guy. He's a great champion, so you can imitate him."

Question: It's quite a compliment.

Mischa Zverev: "Yeah it is. Yeah."

Question: Just out of curiosity, which players have you heard imitate him?

Mischa Zverev: "We all do. Sometimes. Even I did, I think, in practice once in a while. But that's just a common thing, we all do that."

Question: It pumps you up, right?

Mischa Zverev: "Yeah."

"I kind of thought he would be nice to me, especially me being the older player from Adelaide. He just showed no mercy."

Mark Woodforde

Question: What is your first memory of Lleyton Hewitt?

Mark Woodforde: "Oh boy. Probably as a boy, he was a little kid coming from the same city, Adelaide. So I practiced with him quite a bit when he was a youngster, when he was coached by Darren Cahill. Because Darren and I were good mates. In Adelaide, we were always aware of the next generation, you're always trying to cultivate that next breed coming up. So I was a player there for a while, fully aware that Lleyton was coming up. Probably didn't expect him to achieve that level at such a young age. But once he got that initial victory in Adelaide - and I was a victim along the way in that tournament [smiles] - he just improved leaps and bounds. So I always remembered him being like a little kid on the court, meaning you look down there, small stature, his physique was of a youngster. But he just ran and ran and ran. And he made you beat him all the time. He never gave you any cheap, free points. And he was just such a great competitor out there."

Question: Lasting memory of Hewitt, on or off court?

Mark Woodforde: "Probably a testament to his career,

having been number one for a couple of years, holding down that number one as long as he did. And then to accomodate injuries as well as a family, getting married, having kids, traveling with his entourage. His ranking ballooned out to a hundred-whatever it was, and now kind of pushing back into the top forty. I think it shows you don't have to have the biggest serve out there, or the biggest forehand or backhand. Spirit and competitiveness are such tremendous attributes. I think that's the epitome of Lleyton Hewitt."

Question: What was your most memorable match with Hewitt?

Mark Woodforde: "When I finally beat him [smiles]. I think I lost to him, it was a stretch, one of the last years that I played, I think it was like five consecutive tournaments we drew each other first round. I think the first time in that run I kind of was expecting myself to beat him. Didn't. The second time it obviously didn't work out. And then I think I beat myself the next couple of times. Because it was like I knew I had to go through the agony of grinding it out, for the long haul, in a match against him. I really wasn't mentally prepared for it. But I played him all on hard court. So then, finally, the last match we played was in Atlanta on clay. And I actually fancied my chances a little better on the clay, oddly enough, than I did on hard courts."

"And I ended up beating him in three sets I think it was. But I was more prepared to actually hang out there and and stay out there for as long as possible and get the victory. And I think he probably pissed me off enough that I kinda got that fire and drive that 'I can't lose to him five or six times in a row.' I just always remember him being competitive out on the court. He gave you a little latitude. I guess I didn't expect too much of a latitude. I kind of thought he would be nice to me [smiles], especially me being the older player from Adelaide. He just showed no mercy. He still doesn't out on the court. Just watching him last week grind his way through against Bagdhatis (in three sets in Memphis). It's amazing that he still has this want to be out there and play."

Question: Say Rafael Nadal and Lleyton Hewitt switch bodies, switch size and strength, who wins that match?

Mark Woodforde: "Lleyton... Lleyton for sure [smiles]."

Hewitt leads series 5-1

1998	Adelaide	R16	Hewitt	46 76 61
1999	Scottsdale	SF	Hewitt	62 62
1999	Indian Wells Masters	R64	Hewitt	46 62 64
1999	Miami Masters	R128	Hewitt	62 61
1999	Atlanta	R32	Woodforde	26 63 64
2000	Adelaide	R32	Hewitt	63 26 61

About the Author...

Mark "Scoop" Malinowski first started covering professional tennis in 1992 at the Pathmark

Classic exhibition in Mahwah, N.J. He has written about tennis and Biofiled players for such media outlets as Tennis Magazine, Tennis Week Magazine, Tennis Magazine Australia, Ace Magazine (U.K.), www.ATPWorldTour.com, New York Tennis, Florida Tennis, Totally Tennis, Tennis View Magazine, 2014 Australian Open Official Program, among other outlets. He founded the web site www.Tennis-prose.com in 2011.

Scoop has Biofile interviewed Don Budge, Jack Kramer, Roger Federer, Pete Sampras, Ivan Lendl, Chris Evert, Billie Jean King, Tracy Austin, Manuel Santana, Novak Djokovic, Rafael Nadal, Bud Collins, Stefan Edberg, Mats Wilander, Guillermo Vilas, among hundreds of other. His first books about tennis were *"Marcelo Rios: The Man We Barely Knew"* and *"Facing Federer: Symposium of a Champion."*

Special thanks to photo contributors: Chris Chaffee, Gerry Nicholls, Jayita Belcourt, Yonex, Nike Tennis, Onuma Kongasa, Newport Tennis Hall of Fame.

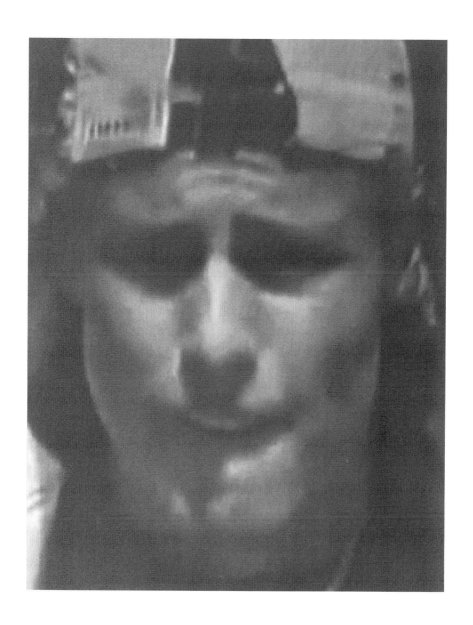

38360685R00155

Made in the USA
Charleston, SC
05 February 2015